GOURMET COOKING *for* Two

CHRISTI SILBAUGH

FRONT TABLE BOOKS

An Imprint of Cedar Fort, Inc.

SPRINGVILLE, UTAH

ISBN: 978-1-4621-1440-5

Published by Front Table Books, an imprint of Cedar Fort, Inc.
2373 W. 700 S., Springville, UT, 84663
Distributed by Cedar Fort, Inc., www.cedarfort.com

LIBRARY OF CONGRESS CATALOGING-IN-PUBLICATION DATA

Silbaugh, Christi.
Gourmet cooking for two / Christi Silbaugh.
      pages cm
Includes index.
ISBN 978-1-4621-1440-5
1. Cooking for two. I. Title.
TX652.S5378 2014
641.5'612—dc 3
                              2014009838

Cover and page design by Erica Dixon and Bekah Claussen
Cover design © 2014 by Lyle Mortimer
Edited by Rachel J. Munk

Printed in the United States of America

10 9 8 7 6 5 4 3 2 1

After our youngest child left the nest, my husband and I down-sized from our traditional suburb home filled with kids, to a loft in the heart of San Diego's historic gaslamp district. Instantly I had a lot of adjustments to make. Being so used to cooking for a large crowd, I found I had to completely reteach myself how to grocery shop and cook for just two people.

I also wanted to spend my newfound extra time to nurture my husband's and my relationship, and to keep the romantic flames burning. As we all know, relationships take work. Life isn't like the movies. There are ups and downs and it takes a whole lot of compromising to make a relationship work. And what about that spark? You know, the one that drew you to each other in the first place. How do you keep that?

As I set out on my journey, I documented what worked and what didn't—both in our kitchen and in our love life, saving the best recipes and romantic tips to share with you. I hope this book encourages and motivates you, in your kitchen and in your love life.

I made all of these recipes to serve two unless otherwise noted.

Enjoy,

Christi

CONTENTS

APPETIZERS

SALADS

SOUPS

MAIN DISHES

SIDE DISHES

DESSERTS

Gourmet Cooking for Two

APPETIZERS

Adult Tater Tots

Avocado Caprese

Bruschetta

Chinese Dumplings

Baked Cream Cheese Rangoons

Crab Cakes

Cucumber Salsa Bites

Cranberry Mistletoe Bites

Fried Mozzarella Bites

Cucumber Wraps

Guacamole

Mushroom Purses

Refreshing Shrimp Bites

Salsa

Deviled Eggs

Spinach Artichoke Dip

Stuffed Mushrooms

Stuffed Tomato Bites

Sweet and Spicy Chicken
Bacon Bites

Spicy Shrimp Bites

ADULT TATER TOTS

This is one of our all-time favorite appetizers. They are worth the extra effort and are the best tasting spuds I have ever had. We call them Adult Tater Tots because they have all the great flavor you loved as a kid, but with the addition of flavors adults love.

Ingredients

1 russet potato

2 Tbsp. potato starch

1 egg

¼ cup minced shallots

1 Tbsp. minced chives

2 slices bacon, chopped

4 oz. Brie cheese

canola oil or other vegetable oil, as needed for frying

salt and pepper to taste

Directions

1. Lightly coat the potato in oil, season with salt and pepper, and pierce it a few times with a fork. Bake at 350 degrees until three-quarters cooked, about 40 minutes. Remove the potato and let it cool to room temperature. Once it is cool enough to handle, peel and grate the potato.

2. In a medium bowl, combine the grated potato, starch, egg, shallots, chives, and salt and pepper to taste. In another small bowl, mix together the chopped bacon and Brie.

3. Fill a one-ounce ring mold, or 1-inch round cookie cutter, halfway with the potato mixture, then place a small scoop of cheese and the bacon mixture in the center and on top. Top with more potato. Press down to firmly compact the potato, then un-mold. Repeat to use all the ingredients.

4. Fill a heavy skillet with enough vegetable oil to cover the tots. Heat the oil at medium-high (approximately 325 degrees), add tots, and cook until golden brown. They will start to float when they are done cooking. Salt and pepper to taste.

 Romantic Tip:

Take a walk together, hand in hand. If you have a cafe, church, or breakfast joint within walking distance, walk there and continue your time together. It is good for the mind, body, and soul.

Christi Silbaugh

AVOCADO CAPRESE

Exchanging cheese for avocado makes for an amazing vegan appetizer that is full of flavor.

Ingredients

2 roma tomatoes

¼ cup chopped fresh basil

2 avocados

salt

freshly ground black pepper

⅓ cup olive oil

balsamic vinegar

1 box of your favorite crackers

Directions

1. Stir together the chopped tomatoes, basil, avocados, salt, pepper, olive oil, and balsamic vinegar.

2. Place 1 tablespoon of the caprese mixture onto your favorite cracker. Serve!

Romantic Tip:
Spend a romantic summer night making wishes on falling stars. Mark the second week in August on your calendar. The earth passes through the Perseid meteor belt around August 12th each year, which usually results in spectacular meteor showers for two to three nights.

Christi Silbaugh

BRUSCHETTA

Bruschetta is an antipasto, or appetizer, from Italy that I absolutely love. I could eat it every day. I keep a big fresh plant of basil in my window planter year round just for this dish.

Ingredients

3 tomatoes
¼ cup chopped fresh basil
2 tsp. minced garlic
¼ cup balsamic vinegar
salt and pepper to taste
½ loaf sourdough baguette
1 Tbsp. olive oil

Directions

1. Core your tomatoes and dice them into tiny pieces. Add them to a bowl.

2. Add the chopped basil and minced garlic. Add the balsamic vinegar and stir. Salt and pepper to taste.

3. Cut the baguette into four slices.

4. Add the olive oil to a skillet and heat over medium heat. Add your baguette slices. Toast them over the olive oil until golden brown and crispy.

5. Top your toast with the tomato basil mixture and serve.

Romantic Tip:

I often hear people say, "I don't dance." I think that is so sad. You don't have to be the best dancer in the world to let loose and boogie down. I often think to myself, "Yes, I do dance; I'm just afraid to do it when people are watching." If you are not one to hop on the dance floor to upbeat music, slow dance with your partner. If you can rock back and forth, you can enjoy a slow dance. Don't be afraid. It's romantic and will bring you closer together.

CHINESE DUMPLINGS

I am a major dumpling fanatic. I love eating them in any way, but savory is my favorite. There is nothing that beats a handmade dumpling, and these fresh noodles call my name. Most people are too scared to try them on their own, but you can do it—they are deceivingly easy to make. With just a little time and patience, you will have your love eating them right out of your hands.

Ingredients

¾ cup flour

¾ cup water, divided

⅓ lb. ground pork

¼ cup chopped cabbage

1 (6–8-oz.) can bamboo shots

1 Tbsp. chopped green onion

⅓ Tbsp. minced fresh ginger

⅓ Tbsp. minced fresh garlic

½ Tbsp. soy sauce

⅓ tsp. salt

⅛ tsp. pepper

⅓ tsp. sesame oil

⅓ tsp. cornstarch

garlic chili sauce (optional)

canola oil for frying

♥ *Romantic Tip:*

Schedule a mini trip apart. I recently went on a short road trip with a couple of girlfriends. I was shocked at how quickly I missed my spouse and how on fire we were when I came home. There is merit to the term "absence makes the heart grow fonder." Every once in a while it's a good way to light the fire again!

Directions

1. Mix the flour and ¼ cup of the water in a large mixing bowl until it is fully incorporated. Knead the dough on a floured surface until smooth. Cover the dough with a damp cloth and let it rest for 30 minutes.

2. Roll the dough into long cylinders about 1½ inches thick, then cut the cylinders into ½-inch pieces. Flatten the pieces with the palm of your hand, forming them into discs. Roll them out to about 2 inches in diameter.

3. Mix all the remaining ingredients together except the ½ cup water.

4. Place a small spoonful of the filling in the center of a disc. Fold the two sides over the center and pleat the edges to seal the filling in.

5. Heat some canola oil in a large pan over medium-high heat. Add the dumplings and fry them until their bottoms are golden brown, about 3 minutes.

6. Carefully add the remaining ½ cup water. Cover and steam the dumplings for 3–5 minutes, until the water has disappeared. Uncover and cook for another 2 minutes over medium-low heat. These are best served with garlic chili sauce.

Christi Silbaugh

BAKED CREAM CHEESE RANGOONS

These little bites of heaven take no time at all, but they taste like they took all day.

Ingredients

6 wonton wrappers
2 oz. cream cheese, softened
½ Tbsp. chopped chives
⅛ tsp. garlic powder
½ Tbsp. melted butter

Directions

1. Preheat the oven to 375 degrees. Spray a mini muffin pan with non-stick spray.

2. Combine the cream cheese, chives, and garlic powder until well mixed.

3. Place about a teaspoon of the cream cheese mixture into the center of each wonton wrapper.

4. Moisten all four sides of a wonton wrapper with a little water. Pinch the wrapper together by bringing the center of each edge to the center of the wonton and pressing it together to make a pouch. Only moisten one wrapper at a time; the edges must be moist in order to stick together.

5. Place the rangoons in your mini muffin pan. Melt the butter and brush lightly on each wonton pouch.

6. Bake for about 15 minutes until golden brown.

 Romantic Tip:

If both of you are looking to increase the romance in your relationship, practice even-day/odd-day romance: On even days it's your turn to be romantic, and on odd days it's your partner's turn. Don't try to one-up each other. True, sincere thoughtfulness will go a long way toward building your relationship.

CRAB CAKES

Forget the artificial fillers! Crab meat is the star of this recipe. It's crispy on the outside, and moist and tender on the inside. A perfect appetizer, or even the main event!

Ingredients

½ lb. crab meat, drained

1 green onion, sliced

⅛ cup plain greek yogurt

½ tsp. vinegar

1 egg

½ tsp. Worcestershire sauce

½ tsp. dry ground mustard

1 tsp. lemon juice

¼ tsp. garlic powder

½ tsp. salt

1 dash cayenne pepper

⅛ cup flour

¼ cup canola oil or other vegetable oil

favorite dipping sauce for serving (optional)

green onions for garnish (optional)

Directions

1. In a large bowl, mix together all the ingredients except the flour and oil.

2. Shape into patties and dust with the flour.

3. Heat the oil in a large skillet over medium heat. When the oil is hot, carefully place the crab cakes, in batches, in the pan and fry for 4–5 minutes, until browned. Carefully flip the crab cakes and fry on the other side until golden brown, about 4 minutes. Serve warm with your preferred sauce.

4. Optional: Sprinkle the top with more sliced green onions for garnish.

Romantic Tip:

What are your spouse's favorite flavors? Is she a chocolate lover? A candy lover? Maybe he loves something savory? Find out and make a dish containing only his or her favorite flavors.

Christi Silbaugh

CUCUMBER SALSA BITES

I call this the perfect party food. You can make a big bowl of this salsa, chop up several cucumbers, and enjoy the party the healthy way!

Ingredients

¼ cup diced sweet onion

1 ripe tomato, diced

⅛ cup chopped cilantro, additional for garnish (optional)

1 garlic clove, minced

1 jalapeño chile, stemmed, seeded, and finely diced

salt and pepper to taste

1 cucumber, peeled and sliced

Directions

1. In a small bowl, mix together the onion, tomato, cilantro, minced garlic, and jalapeño. Stir and add salt and pepper to taste.

2. Place your sliced cucumbers on a plate, top with salsa, and serve.

3. Garnish your plate with cilantro if desired.

 Romantic Tip:

Pamper your sweetie during the big game—or if sports aren't his thing, do it during his favorite show. It'll make him feel taken care of and loved.

CRANBERRY MISTLETOE BITES

These are perfect for any holiday party. When I served them my husband said, "Oh look, they look like mistletoe!" So now we call them mistletoe appetizers!

Ingredients

½ cup cranberries
¼ cup agave nectar
¼ cup granulated sugar
8 crackers of your choice
4 oz. Brie cheese
2 Tbsp. cranberry sauce
fresh mint for garnish
(optional)

Directions

1. Rinse the cranberries and place them in a medium bowl.

2. Heat the agave nectar in a small saucepan until warm. Pour over the cranberries when the agave nectar is warm, not hot, or the cranberries may pop. Cool, cover, and let soak in the refrigerator overnight.

3. Drain the cranberries in a colander and place the sugar in a large bowl. Add the cranberries in 2 batches and roll around until lightly coated in sugar. Place on a baking sheet until dry, about 1 hour.

4. Assemble your crackers with one slice of Brie, a light layer of cranberry sauce, and 3 sugared cranberries. Garnish with fresh mint sprigs if desired.

Romantic Tip:

Set aside time to just be spontaneous. Go out to a movie, dinner, dancing, or even to a live show. Whatever floats your boat. The time you spend will bring you closer together and will refuel you for the rest of the week.

Christi Silbaugh

FRIED MOZZARELLA BITES

Using fresh mozzarella, you get a dish that is far better than any restaurant appetizer.

Ingredients

1 lb. fresh mozzarella balls

1 egg

⅛ cup milk

½ cup flour

½ cup bread crumbs

¼ tsp. sea salt

1 Tbsp. grated Parmesan

1½ cups canola oil

salt and pepper to taste

1 cup marinara sauce

♥ *Romantic Tip:*

Buy a lottery ticket. Give it to your partner with a little note attached, "I hit the jackpot when I met you!"

Directions

1. Drain the mozzarella cheese from its liquid and place it on a paper towel.

2. In a bowl, whisk together the egg and milk.

3. Put the egg mixture and flour in separate wide, shallow bowls. Combine the bread crumbs with the salt and Parmesan in another wide, shallow bowl.

4. Roll the cheese in the flour, dip into the egg mixture, and coat with the bread crumbs, shaking off the excess after each step. Repeat the breading process for each cheese piece.

5. In a large, deep sauté pan over medium-high heat, pour the oil to a depth of 3 inches and heat to 375 degrees on a deep-fryer thermometer.

6. Working in batches, fry the cheese for about one minute, or until golden brown.

7. Transfer the fried cheese to a paper towel lined plate and season with salt and pepper. Place the cheese on a wire rack set over a baking sheet, keeping it warm in the oven while frying the remaining cheese.

8. Serve with warm marinara sauce.

CUCUMBER WRAPS

I am always looking for healthy appetizers to have ready for my man while I am cooking dinner. It never fails—the minute I start cooking dinner he wanders in and opens the fridge, looking for something to calm his stomach that the good-smelling kitchen has awakened. My solution is to have fruits and veggies available. This dish tempts his taste buds and gets him ready for the main event.

Ingredients

1 English cucumber

2 Roma tomatoes

a few sprigs fresh dill

2 Tbsp. cream cheese, softened

Directions

1. Using a mandolin or a very sharp knife, slice your cucumber very thin lengthwise.

2. Cut the core out of the tomatoes and cut them into long, thin slices.

3. On each cucumber, spread about one teaspoon cream cheese, a sprig of fresh dill, and a slice of tomato.

4. Roll them up and keep them in place with a toothpick.

Romantic Tip:

Are you just maintaining your relationship? Or are you nourishing it, growing it, and allowing it to thrive? Unfortunately, we are human, and too much of the same thing gets boring. Spice it up! Don't just maintain your relationship. Do something that will make your partner feel special and loved.

GUACAMOLE

This is my all-time favorite way to make guacamole. Creamy and chunky at the same time, just as it should be.

Ingredients

½ cup sweet onion finely chopped

2 garlic clove, minced

2 jalapeño chiles, stemmed, seeded and finely diced

1 lime, juiced

3 avocados, diced into ½-inch pieces

sea salt to taste

chopped cilantro (optional)

Directions

1. Put the onion, garlic, chiles, lime juice, and avocados in a bowl.

2. Use a large serving fork, mix up the ingredients. Then press the fork around the sides of the bowl, mashing the avocados. This will make a chunky guacamole.

3. Add sea salt to taste. If you like cilantro, by all means add it. We love it, but I know for some people it is a cringe ingredient.

Romantic Tip:

My husband once surprised me on our vacation. He picked a private spot to take me away from our friends and family for some "us" time. Sometimes vacations can be stressful and over-planned. Plan a romantic date on your vacation, some time for just the two of you to connect.

MUSHROOM PURSES

I think one-bite foods are very romantic. They make everything look gourmet and taste like an explosion in your mouth. These mushroom purses are one of my husband's favorites.

Ingredients

1 leek, washed thoroughly and chopped (see step 2)

2 Tbsp. olive oil

½ lb. sliced mushrooms

½ Tbsp. finely chopped fresh thyme

salt and pepper to taste

⅛ cup white wine

wonton wrappers

2 oz. Fontina cheese

2 Tbsp. butter

fresh chives

Romantic Tip:

Spend time just spending time together. Turn that TV off and entertain each other the way your grandparents did. There is a lot to be said for "old school romance."

Directions

1. Preheat the oven to 400 degrees.

2. To prepare the leek: Cut away the blue/green leaves on top and trim the base. Peel away the first layer. Slice the leek into ¼-inch rings from top to bottom. Push through each sliced ring, drop them into a strainer, and rinse with cold running water. Place the strainer in a bowl and fill with cold water. Let stand so the sand/grit falls to bottom. Throw out the sandy water and rinse the leek again in cold running water. Shake off the remaining water and set aside to dry for a few minutes.

3. Sauté the leeks over medium heat in 1 tablespoon of olive oil until soft, about 5 minutes. Do not brown. Remove from the skillet and place in a large bowl.

4. Remove the stems from the mushrooms and chop. Add the remaining 1 tablespoon olive oil to the skillet. When hot, add enough of the mushrooms to cover the bottom of the pan. Sauté over medium-high heat for about 5 minutes, or until mushrooms are soft.

5. Return the leeks to the skillet with the mushrooms. Add the thyme, salt, pepper, and wine. Cook over high heat, stirring until all liquid is reduced to a syrupy consistency. Set aside.

6. Lay out a wonton wrapper and place one tablespoon of the leek mixture in the center of the rectangle. Top this with 1 teaspoon Fontina cheese. Tie the pastry closed with a chive and repeat until all of the mushroom mixture is gone.

7. Place the pastry on a baking sheet or baking dish sprayed with cooking spray. Melt the butter and brush it on top of the prepared purses. Bake for 15 minutes or until golden brown. Remove from the oven.

Christi Silbaugh

REFRESHING SHRIMP BITES

The avocado pineapple salsa and refreshing cucumber make these shrimp bites so light and refreshing.

Ingredients

½ Tbsp. vegetable oil
10 large shrimp or prawns
½ tsp. minced shallots
½ tsp. chopped garlic
½ Tbsp. lime juice
½ Tbsp. brown sugar
½ Tbsp. vegetable stock
½ Tbsp. butter
salt and pepper to taste
1 cucumber, peeled and sliced ½-in. thick

avocado pineapple salsa:

½ cup fresh chopped pineapple
1 tsp. chopped red bell pepper
1 tsp. chopped yellow bell pepper
1 tsp. chopped green bell pepper
1 tsp. chopped green onion
1 tsp. chopped cilantro
1 avocado, diced
4 leaves mint, chopped
juice of ½ a lime

Directions

1. Start by making the avocado pineapple salsa: Peel, core and grill the pineapple. Once it is cooked, chop it up.

2. Chop up all peppers, onion, and cilantro, and add them to the pineapple.

3. Mix the avocado in gently and garnish with the chopped mint leaves. Set in the fridge while you finish the shrimp.

4. Heat the oil in a frying pan over medium-high heat.

5. Sauté and season the shrimp and add the shallots and garlic.

6. Deglaze the pan with the lime juice. Add the brown sugar, vegetable stock, and butter. Reduce the liquid until it thickens into a caramel-like sauce. Salt and pepper the glaze to taste.

7. Set out your sliced cucumbers and make a cup out of them, scooping out a small portion of the seeded area. Top your sliced cucumber cups with pineapple avocado salsa.

8. Next, add the glazed shrimp. Garnish with mint and cilantro and serve! This dish can be served hot or cold.

Romantic Tip:

If your significant other wants to adopt a healthier lifestyle, support them. Join in the battle. Two against one gives you much better odds at winning!

Christi Silbaugh

SALSA

Not only is this salsa amazing and bursting with flavor, but it couldn't be easier or quicker to make.

Ingredients

14 oz. canned whole tomatoes (peeled) with juice

10 oz. canned diced tomatoes with green chilies

⅛ cup onion chopped

1 jalapeño chile, stemmed, seeded, and finely diced

¼ cup cilantro

2 Tbsp. lime juice

¼ tsp. sea salt

¼ tsp. cumin

¼ tsp. sugar

Directions

1. Add all the ingredients to a food processor. Pulse the mixture until it reaches your desired consistency.

Romantic Tip:

Write your partner a note about your most memorable time together. It will spark your memory and get the creative juices flowing. You can even spray the note with your favorite perfume or cologne for a romantic touch.

Christi Silbaugh

DEVILED EGGS

Deviled eggs are the "must have" appetizer in our home during the holidays. They are great because you can make them the day before, then serve them while you are spending time with your love.

Ingredients

4 eggs, hard-boiled and peeled

⅛ cup mayonnaise

½ Tbsp. yellow mustard

salt and pepper to taste

½ tsp. paprika

½ Tbsp. dill pickle, finely chopped

Directions

1. Halve the eggs lengthwise. Remove the yolks and place them in a small bowl. Set the egg whites aside.

2. Whisk together the yolks, mayonnaise, and mustard. Add salt and pepper to taste.

3. Fill the egg whites evenly with the yolk mixture. I like to use a pastry decorator to put the yolks in. It helps to smash them at the same time. Garnish with the paprika and pickles. Store covered in the refrigerator.

Romantic Tip:

Resolve to become more romantic and you will. Get a book on romancing your partner. Do one romantic thing a day and watch them start doing it in return.

Christi Silbaugh

SPINACH ARTICHOKE DIP

One of our favorite casual appetizers is this Spinach and Artichoke Dip. It's easy to throw together and is so yummy! It's pure comfort food. You can dip veggies, chips, or crackers.

Ingredients

4 oz. cream cheese

¼ cup sour cream

⅛ cup mayonnaise

½ cup chopped fresh spinach leaves

1 small can or jar plain, non-marinated artichoke hearts, chopped

¼ tsp. garlic salt

½ tsp. chili powder

⅛ cup shredded mozzarella cheese, plus more to sprinkle on top

⅛ cup shredded cheddar cheese, plus more to sprinkle on top

⅛ cup shredded Parmesan cheese, plus more to sprinkle on top

Directions

1. Preheat the oven to broil.

2. Mix all the ingredients in a baking dish and sprinkle the extra cheese on top.

3. Broil for 5–10 minutes, until the cheese is brown and the dip is bubbly on the sides.

 Romantic Tip:

Have a romantic night in. Cut out stars from construction paper; or, if you want to recycle, cut them out of paper grocery bags. If you have time you can even paint them. Hang the stars by fishing line from the ceiling in different lengths, so some of the stars will hang lower than the others. Light candles and ask your significant other to join you for an evening of dancing under the stars.

Christi Silbaugh

STUFFED MUSHROOMS

Be prepared for these mushrooms to be devoured. Although they are made as an appetizer, they'll quickly become the main event.

Ingredients

8 button mushrooms

1 oz. cream cheese

1 Tbsp. jalapeño chile, stemmed, seeded, and finely diced

2 Tbsp. freshly grated Parmesan cheese

1 Tbsp. crumbled Gorgonzola cheese

Directions

1. Remove the stems from the mushrooms and set aside.

2. Chop the mushroom stems in a food processor. Add the remaining ingredients and process until smooth.

3. Place the mushroom caps on a baking sheet.

4. Pipe the mixture into the mushroom caps.

5. Bake in a preheated 350 degree oven for 20 minutes.

6. May be served warm or at room temperature.

 Romantic Tip:

Don't get stuck in a rut. I once heard a saying, "Men, never stop dating your wives. Women, never stop flirting with your husbands." This is great advice, and I'll take it one step further. Men, don't just go out to a movie on Saturday like you usually do. Call your partner from work and formally ask her on a date. Women, dress up, put on that special perfume, and get dolled up for your man. Make sure to flirt with him all night too!

STUFFED TOMATO BITES

These little one bite wonders are more than just pretty to look at. Pop one in your mouth, and you'll experience a parade of flavors that will keep you coming back for more.

Ingredients

6 cherry tomatoes

1 oz. cream cheese

2 tsp. freshly chopped basil, additional for garnish

¼ tsp. freshly chopped chives, additional for garnish

⅛ tsp. salt

1 dash pepper

Directions

1. Cut the tops off the cherry tomatoes and take out about half of the insides. You may have to cut a little off the bottom of them to get them to stand up.

2. In a mixer, or by hand with a whisk, add the cream remaining ingredients. Mix until thoroughly blended and smooth.

3. Pipe the cream cheese mixture into the hollow tomatoes. I do this by putting the cheese mixture into a ziploc bag and cutting off one corner. Squeeze out the cheese mixture into the cherry tomatoes.

4. Garnish with chives and basil.

 Romantic Tip:

While your partner is showering, sneak in and write "I love you" on the steamed mirror.

SWEET AND SPICY CHICKEN BACON BITES

These little bites of heaven are the perfect combination of sweet and spicy.

Ingredients

½ lb. boneless and skinless chicken breasts

⅓ lb. sliced bacon

⅓ cup brown sugar

1 Tbsp. chili powder

Directions

1. Preheat the oven to 350 degrees.

2. Cut the chicken breasts into 1-inch cubes. Cut each bacon slice into thirds. Wrap each chicken cube with bacon and secure with a toothpick.

3. In a small bowl, stir together the brown sugar and chili powder. Dredge the wrapped chicken in the brown sugar mixture.

4. Coat a rack and broiler pan with non-stick cooking spray. Place the chicken wrap on rack in broiler pan.

5. Bake 350 for 30–35 minutes or until the bacon is crisp.

Romantic Tip:

Choose happiness each and every day. Happiness in love comes from the inside, and unless both of you choose to be happy, no amount of gestures will make a difference.

Christi Silbaugh

SPICY SHRIMP BITES

Everything is better with bacon! These scrumptious appetizers are full of all things yummy. Enjoy the rich flavor of the shrimp and the kick of jalapeño, finished with salty, crunchy bacon. Dig in!

Ingredients

6 jumbo shrimp

1 clove garlic, minced

½ Tbsp. freshly minced parsley

1 Tbsp. jalapeño chiles, stemmed, seeded, and finely diced

2 oz. Gorgonzola cheese, crumbled

1 oz. plain Greek yogurt

3 bacon strips

Directions

1. Preheat your oven to broil.

2. Peel and devein the shrimp, then butterfly them by slicing down the back, ¾ of the way through each shrimp. Rinse and set aside in an ice filled bowl.

3. Mince the garlic, parsley and jalapeño chiles, then mix with the Gorgonzola cheese and Greek yogurt in small bowl until well combined.

4. Fill each shrimp with one ½ tablespoon of cheese mixture. Wrap each shrimp with ½ slice of bacon.

5. Place the shrimp on a grill pan or a cookie sheet topped with a cooling rack. This will allow the bacon juice to run into the pan below. Broil on high for 6 minutes.

6. You can serve with toothpicks, or on a cute serving tray. You can also serve over pasta or rice.

Romantic Tip:

Decorate on special occasions. Use craft paper or heart doilies and hang them all over the house. It is a cute romantic gesture that is sure to make your partner smile.

Christi Silbaugh

ANGRY CABBAGE SALAD

Cabbage has the fewest calories and the least fat of any vegetable. This salad takes more energy to digest than the calories it provides your body, so it's a great detox salad.

Ingredients

2 Tbsp. soy sauce

½ tsp. mustard seeds

½ tsp. cumin

1 bay leaf

½ tsp. ground tumeric

½ tsp. curry powder

½ cinnamon stick

½ sweet onion, sliced

1 serrano pepper, sliced

1 red pepper, sliced

½ head of cabbage, shredded

½ Tbsp. red chili paste

sea salt to taste

Directions

1. Spray a skillet with cooking spray.

2. Heat the skillet to medium-high heat and add the soy sauce to the skillet. Add the mustard seeds, cumin, bay leaf, turmeric, curry powder, and cinnamon and fry for 30 seconds without burning.

3. Add the onions and peppers and cook for another minute.

4. Add the cabbage. Stir and cook until it becomes a little wilted.

5. Add the red chili paste and stir. Add sea salt to taste. Serve hot or cold!

Romantic Tip:

Before you meet up with your significant other tonight, adjust your mood to the way you want them to feel. Make your spouse feel alluring and interesting at home by creating a sexy atmosphere, and they will always be excited to come home to you, guaranteed!

Christi Silbaugh

CHEESE, WALNUT, & PEAR SALAD

Don't be afraid of gorgonzola! The cheese mixed with pears and walnuts will make your taste buds dance.

Ingredients

2 Tbsp. walnuts

2 cups mixed super greens (chard, arugula, spinach)

1 pear, peeled, cored, and sliced thin

1 pomegranate, seeds only

2 Tbsp. crumbled gorgonzola cheese

olive oil

balsamic vinegar

Directions

1. Start out by toasting the walnuts in a cast iron skillet for a few minutes, stirring constantly.

2. Fill a salad bowl with your mixed greens. Top with the sliced pear and the pomegranate seeds.

3. Top your salad with the gorgonzola cheese and the walnuts.

4. Drizzle a little bit of olive oil and balsamic vinegar on top.

5. Serve immediately.

Romantic Tip:

Be your partner's number one fan. Even men, who appear to be strong and independent, need to know and feel that their partners believe in him. The truth is, men and women alike are stronger and better able to meet challenges when they have support and encouragement.

CONFETTI KALE SALAD WITH DIJON DRESSING

The light taste of these leafy greens combined with the sweetness of red bell peppers and sweet onion will blow you away.

Ingredients

6 kale leaves

1 cup chopped red bell pepper

¼ cup olive oil

2 Tbsp. finely chopped sweet onion

1 Tbsp. agave nectar

1 Tbsp. Dijon mustard

½ lemon, juiced

1 tsp. sea salt

½ tsp. freshly ground black pepper

½ Tbsp. garlic, minced

1 tsp. ground mustard

Directions

1. Wash and dry the kale and then strip the leaves from the stem. Discard the stem. Rip the leaves into bite-sized pieces. Add the bell peppers to the kale.

2. For the dressing: Place the remaining ingredients in a high-powered blender and blend until smooth.

3. Pour over the salad and toss. Serve and enjoy. This salad will keep in a sealed container in the fridge for up to 3 days.

Romantic Tip:

You know what I like? Getting old-fashioned mail. These days, it seems like all I get in my mailbox is a big pile of advertisements. Every once in a while I am surprised with something legit. It's a huge surprise when my husband sends me a letter—it lets me know I am on his mind.

Christi Silbaugh

CREAMY CUCUMBER SALAD

With just 6 ingredients and 5 minutes you can have this refreshing salad, perfect for a spring or summer meal.

Ingredients

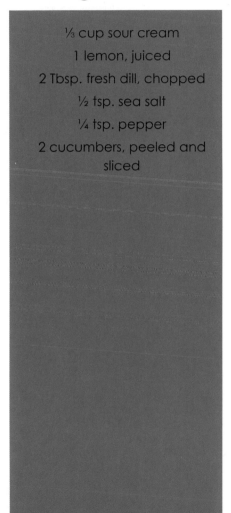

⅓ cup sour cream

1 lemon, juiced

2 Tbsp. fresh dill, chopped

½ tsp. sea salt

¼ tsp. pepper

2 cucumbers, peeled and sliced

Directions

1. In a medium bowl, combine the sour cream, lemon juice, and dill. Season with salt and pepper and whisk well to combine.

2. Add the cucumbers to the bowl and toss to coat.

3. Garnish with more dill, if desired. Serve or refrigerate, covered, up to 4 hours.

Romantic Tip:

Pretend you're going on a first date. Show up at the door with flowers, all dressed up, with your car washed and cleaned. You can even re-create your first date!

GINGER-SESAME CHICKEN SALAD

This is one of my favorite things to make a day ahead and pack in my husband's lunch. The cabbage stays firm and it gives my husband a gourmet meal away from home.

Ingredients

¼ cup soy sauce

3 Tbsp. fresh ginger minced

¼ cup canola oil

2 Tbsp. hoisin sauce

1 Tbsp. sesame oil

1 tsp. sriracha

1 tsp. salt

2 chicken breasts

¼ cup red wine vinegar

¼ cup chopped green onions

For the salad:

1 head cabbage

4 carrots, peeled and jullienned

3 green onions, thinly sliced

1 tsp. sesame seeds, toasted

½ cup slivered almonds

Romantic Tip:

Have a video game night with your man. Show him his likes are just as important as yours.

Directions

1. Whisk together the first seven ingredients (through the salt) to make the marinade.

2. With a meat pounder, pound the breasts to a uniform thickness. This will allow them to cook more evenly and will also help tenderize the meat.

3. Put the two chicken breasts in a gallon sized ziploc bag and add 4 tablespoons of the marinade to the chicken. Allow the flattened chicken breasts to marinate for 30 minutes. You will be using the remainder of the marinade to make the dressing.

4. For the dressing: Add the red wine vinegar and sliced green onions to the reserved marinade.

5. Cook the chicken. You can grill, bake, or pan fry it. I like to pan fry with 1 tablespoon grapeseed oil and salt and pepper. Cook over medium-high heat for 5 minutes on the first side, flip over, and cook for another 4 minutes.

6. In a large bowl, add the cabbage, carrots, green onions, half of the sesame seeds, and half of the almonds. Add the chicken and mix together. Add just enough of the dressing to coat the salad lightly and toss together.

7. Distribute the salad to 4–6 plates. Re-whisk the dressing and drizzle a little over each salad. Garnish with the remaining almonds and sesame seeds.

Christi Silbaugh

SHAVED ASPARAGUS SALAD

This nice and simple cold salad is very low calorie, but is also full of flavor.

Ingredients

12 oz. asparagus, trimmed

2 Tbsp. soy sauce

1 Tbsp. fresh lemon juice

sea salt to taste

black pepper to taste

1 cup chopped romaine lettuce

Directions

1. Shave the asparagus into long, thin strands, using a vegetable peeler or mandolin. Soak the strands in a large bowl of ice water for one hour. Drain well and dry with paper towels.

2. To make the dressing, combine the soy sauce, lemon juice, salt, and pepper to taste in a small bowl. Whisk until blended.

3. Pour the dressing over the asparagus and toss well. Arrange over a bed of lettuce. Serve immediately.

 Romantic Tip:

Do something unexpected for your spouse, even it is something little. If she gets up at the crack of dawn to go to work one cold morning, slip outside, start the car for her, and turn on the heat so it will be nice and warm when she leaves.

Christi Silbaugh

SWEET AND SPICY CARROT CUCUMBER SALAD

This is a crisp, refreshing salad with a kick.

Ingredients

1 cucumber, thinly sliced lengthwise

1 carrot, thinly sliced lengthwise

½ cup green onion, sliced

2 Tbsp. rice vinegar

1 Tbsp. mirin

½ Tbsp. sesame oil

¼ tsp. chili paste

Directions

1. Combine all the ingredients in a bowl and let it marinade for 30 minutes.

2. Serve in two individual serving dishes. It's tasty and healthy!

 Romantic Tip:

We usually wait until the weekend to go to the grocery store for our big purchases. I walk to the store almost every day, but on weekends I pick up the heavy items like detergent, beverages, and anything heavy like a bag of potatoes. Carrying those by myself for 6 blocks is not fun, even though I have done it many times. One time I decided to go get them myself, just as a nice gesture for my hubby. Eliminating one chore from anyone's day is always nice. Try eliminating one of your love's chores today.

Salads

TACO SALAD

This is a delicious, healthy vegetarian taco salad. Easily add your favorite meat for the carnivores in your life.

Ingredients

1 cup refried beans

¼ cup shredded cheddar cheese

2 cups chopped romaine lettuce

½ cup salsa

¼ cup guacamole

¼ cup sour cream or plain Greek yogurt

tortilla chips (optional)

Directions

1. Divide the following between 2 plates: Heat up the refried beans and add ½ cup to the center of each plate. Sprinkle the cheese on top.

2. Surround the beans with lettuce. Each plate should have 1 cup of tightly packed, chopped romaine lettuce.

3. Pour the salsa around the beans.

4. Top with guacamole and sour cream, or plain Greek yogurt.

5. Optional: surround your plate with corn tortilla chips.

Romantic Tip:

On one of those extra busy days, skip the kitchen duties. Bring home great take-out and light some candles for a private picnic in your house. Wear something romantic, or get all dressed up for your significant other!

Christi Silbaugh

THAI CHICKEN SALAD

This salad makes you forget you are eating salad at all! It's full of flavor and is very satisfying.

Ingredients

1½ cups shredded cabbage and carrots (coleslaw blend)

½ cup papaya, sliced

½ cup cucumber, sliced

1 cup baby bok choy, chopped into small pieces

1 red chili pepper, diced

⅛ cup mint, chopped

¼ cup slivered almonds

2 chicken breasts, cooked and shredded

for the dressing:

1 lime, juiced

1 Tbsp. olive oil

1 Tbsp. soy sauce

1 Tbsp. agave nectar

1 Tbsp. peanut butter

½ tsp. fish sauce

1 pinch red pepper flakes

Directions

1. It is important to cut the veggies and papaya into a similar size. It helps them dance on your taste buds as the flavors blend together and bounce off each other.

2. Add all the salad ingredients except the chicken to a large bowl and toss.

3. Add the chicken to the salad bowl. In a smaller bowl mix all the dressing ingredients together.

4. Pour the dressing over salad and toss well.

5. Serve cold.

Romantic Tip:

Help your significant other be the best person he or she can be. Whether it is exercising together, eating right together, skipping dessert together, or whatever it may be, you'll both be more likely to succeed if you work together.

Christi Silbaugh

WEDGE SALAD

This classic wedge of iceberg lettuce is topped with a variety of veggies and a creamy dressing.

Ingredients

½ head iceburg lettuce

blue cheese dressing

¼ cup trimmed and chopped sugar snap peas

¼ cup peeled, seeded and diced tomatoes

¼ cup chopped green onions

¼ cup carrots, peeled and diced

¼ cup chopped celery

Directions

1. Cut your head of lettuce in half, making two wedges.

2. Top each wedge with the dressing, then top with chopped veggies.

Romantic Tip:

Do something nice for someone. Doing nice things for others brings positive light into all your relationships. Is there someone at work you'd like to befriend but don't know how? Is there a neighbor who once said, "I'd love to have you over for a drink sometime" but never followed through? Try a simple gesture to break the ice. Buy them a little something or offer to do them a helpful favor. You will be impressing your partner and brightening someone's day at the same time!

Christi Silbaugh

BEAN AND BACON SOUP

This soup sticks to your ribs and keeps you satisfied for hours on end.

Ingredients

¼ lb. bacon, diced

1 large sweet onion, diced

1 garlic clove, minced

1 cup cooked red kidney beans (any cooked bean will work fine).

1 sprig thyme

½ tsp. tarragon

1 bay leaf

4 cups chicken broth

Directions

1. Sauté the bacon in a large pot until it just starts to crisp.

2. Add the onions and sweat them for five minutes.

3. Add the remaining ingredients and slowly cook over low heat for one hour.

4. Remove the bay leaf and thyme sprig and serve.

Romantic Tip:

When your love is sick, take some extra time to make things as comfortable as possible for them. Make sure there are plenty of liquids available, and offer to put together a simple meal like toast and soup. If your partner is like me, they won't ask for help, so just do it so they don't have to.

Christi Silbaugh

BLACK BEAN SOUP

I make a large pot of this soup before the weekend. When we need something to fill us up, I just heat up two bowls of this healthy spicy soup. It satisfies our hunger for hours on end, without affecting our waistlines. Having this pre-made really frees up time so we can just focus on each other.

Ingredients

3 Tbsp. olive oil

1 white onion, chopped

3 garlic cloves, minced

1 celery stalk diced

2 jalapeño peppers, minced

1 carrot, finely chopped

4 tsp. cumin

4 tsp. chili powder

2 tsp. sea salt

½ tsp. black pepper

32 oz. cooked or canned black beans

32 oz. chicken broth

3 Tbsp. fresh lime juice

optional garnishes:
Greek yogurt or sour cream,
cheddar cheese, parsley,
cilantro, tortilla chips

Directions

1. In a large pan, sauté in the oil the onion, garlic, celery, peppers, and carrots until tender, about 5 minutes.

2. Add the cumin, chili powder, salt, and pepper to coat the onion mixture.

3. Add the beans and chicken broth. Reduce to a low boil until the sauce thickens, about 30 minutes.

4. Add the fresh lime juice and serve with garnishes of your choice.

Romantic Tip:

"I like you. I love you. I'm proud of you." Say and mean these three phrases often—affirmation through clear communication is the key to healthy relationships.

CHICKEN POT PIE

A delicious chicken pie made from scratch with carrots, peas, and celery.

Ingredients

1½ cups chicken broth

1 cup whole milk

1 bay leaf

⅛ cup corn starch

⅛ cup cold water

1½ cups cooked chicken breast, cut into chunks

½ cup frozen or raw carrots, peeled and diced

½ cup frozen or raw peas

¼ tsp. thyme

¼ tsp. sage

⅛ tsp. freshly ground black pepper

½ tsp. sea salt

puff pastry, thawed if frozen

1 egg

1 Tbsp. water

Romantic Tip:

Public Display of Attention (the other PDA). Proudly and sincerely compliment, dote over, and affirm your significant other in front of others.

Directions

1. Place the chicken broth, milk, and bay leaf in a medium to large soup pot over medium heat.

2. Slowly heat the broth and milk, being careful not to heat too quickly.

3. Meanwhile, mix the cold water and cornstarch in a small bowl. Slowly whisk the slurry into the milk and broth mixture. Bring to a boil, stirring constantly. Reduce heat.

4. Add the cooked chicken, vegetables, and all seasonings. Simmer for 20 minutes.

5. Preheat the oven to 400 degrees.

6. Place the cooked stew into a baking dish or individual baking bowls.

7. Roll out your puff pastry and cut it into your desired shape to cover your baking dish. Then place them back in the freezer for 10 minutes. If you have multiple shapes, separate them with parchment paper.

8. Place the puff pastry on top of your dish or dishes. Cut a hole to allow steam to escape.

9. Brush the top of the pastry with an egg wash (one egg and tablespoon of water). Bake for 20–25 minutes.

Christi Silbaugh

CLAM CHOWDER

A delicious traditional cream-based chowder.

Ingredients

¼ cup minced onion

¼ cup chopped celery

¼ cup diced carrots

½ cup cubed potatoes

6 (½-oz.) clams, juice included

¼ cup water

¼ cup butter

1 Tbsp. flour

½ cup heavy whipping cream

1 cup whole milk

1 strip bacon

½ Tbsp. red wine vinegar

1 tsp. sea salt

freshly ground black pepper

green onions for garnish
(optional)

Directions

1. Chop the onions, celery, and carrots into the same size.

2. Chop the potatoes to double the size of your veggies.

3. Drain the leftover juice from the clams into a large pot over the onion, celery, potatoes, and carrots. Add the water and cook over medium heat until tender.

4. Add the butter to the veggies over medium heat. Whisk in flour until smooth.

5. Whisk in the cream and milk, and stir constantly until thick and smooth.

6. Stir in the vegetables, bacon, and clam juice. Heat through but do not boil.

7. Stir in the clams just before serving. If they cook too much they will get tough.

8. When the clams are heated through, stir in the vinegar, and season with salt and pepper. Garnish with green onions and serve.

Romantic Tip:

Revisit a first date or first meeting place. Reminisce about what brought you together, what you have learned since, and what you're looking forward to together.

Christi Silbaugh

CORN CHOWDER

The flavor of this soup is off the hook. And it's low calorie. You can omit the bacon bits for an even healthier meal.

Ingredients

1½ cups fresh corn

2½ cups chicken broth

2 slices bacon, more for garnish

½ Tbsp. extra virgin olive oil

½ sweet onion, finely chopped

1 garlic clove, chopped

1 poblano chile, chopped

1 carrot, finely chopped

1 celery stalk, chopped

1 russet potato, peeled and diced

salt and pepper to taste

1 Tbsp. corn starch

1 Tbsp. lime juice

½ Tbsp. Italian seasoning

optional garnishes:

cotija cheese, crumbled

cilantro, minced

Romantic Tip:

Read poetry together. Then talk about the poem and what you each got from it.

Directions

1. Place ¾ cup of the corn into a medium pot with the broth and simmer for 40 minutes.

2. Puree with a hand immersion blender. Strain through a sieve.

3. Place the corn-infused stock back into the pot and set aside. Discard the rest of the puree.

4. In a large pan, cook the bacon until crisp. Remove from the pan, drain, and set onto paper towels so it will continue to drain.

5. In the same pan you cooked the bacon in, add olive oil to the grease and sauté the onion, garlic, poblano chile, carrots, celery, and potatoes. Sauté for 5–7 minutes or until the vegetables begin to soften.

6. Stir in the remaining corn kernels and season with salt and pepper.

7. Sprinkle the vegetables with the corn starch and stir for about 3 minutes. Continue to stir while adding the lime juice to avoid any lumps forming. Add the stock until fully incorporated. Add the Italian seasoning or any of your favorite minced herbs.

8. Allow the mixture to come to a hard simmer for about 5 minutes, or until the mixture thickens. Reduce the heat to medium-low and season to taste with salt and pepper.

9. To serve, top with a sprinkle of Cotija cheese, cilantro, and crispy bacon. Dig in!

CROCK-POT CREAMY CHICKEN CHILI

This chili is a dream. It's easy to make, easily changeable, and so thick and luscious.

Ingredients

1 cup cooked black beans

2 chicken breasts

1 cup fresh or frozen corn kernels

1 (10-oz.) can diced tomato with green chiles

1 tsp. parsley

1 tsp. basil

1 tsp. dill

1 tsp. chives

1 tsp. garlic powder

1 tsp. onion powder

½ tsp. sea salt

½ tsp. pepper

1 tsp. cumin

1 Tbsp. chili powder

8 oz. cream cheese

optional garnish: sour cream or greek yogurt, corn chips

Directions

1. Drain and rinse the black beans.

2. Place the chicken at bottom of a crock-pot, then pour in the corn, rotel, and black beans. Top with the seasonings.

3. Cover with a lid and cook on low for 6–8 hours.

4. Stir the cream cheese into the chili.

5. Use two forks to shred the chicken. Stir together and serve.

 Romantic Tip:

Write a poem or love note to your partner and sneak it into their work bag, or leave it in another place where they will not expect it.

Christi Silbaugh

CROCK-POT ENCHILADA SOUP

A Mexican dinner that's ready to cook in 10 minutes.

Ingredients

3 Tbsp. butter

2 Tbsp. flour

½ cup chicken broth

2 cups milk

10 oz. enchilada sauce (canned or fresh)

15 oz. cooked or canned black beans

1 (14.5-oz.) can diced tomatoes with chiles

½ cup chopped onion

2 chicken breasts

1 cup Monterey Jack cheese

sour cream or plain Greek yogurt

tortilla chips

Romantic Tip:
Create a little portable box and put a bunch of your partner's favorite things inside.

Directions

1. Melt the butter in a saucepan over medium-low heat.

2. Stir in the flour until smooth and bubbly.

3. Remove from the heat and add the chicken broth and ½ cup milk, a little at a time, stirring to keep smooth.

4. Return to the heat. Bring the sauce to a gentle boil and cook, stirring constantly, until it thickens.

5. In a large bowl, whisk together the enchilada sauce and chicken broth mixture. Gradually whisk in the remaining milk until smooth. Set aside.

6. In a crock-pot, combine the drained beans, tomatoes, onion, and chicken breasts. Pour the sauce mixture over these ingredients. Cover and cook on low heat for 6–8 hours or on high for 3–4 hours.

7. When you are ready to serve, remove the chicken and shred into bite-sized pieces. Add the chicken back into the soup and mix together.

8. Top with the cheese and serve. You can garnish your soup with whatever you like. Popular toppings are cheese, sour cream, chips, avocado, and cilantro.

FRENCH ONION SOUP

A fabulous meal for a cold winter day.

Ingredients

2 Tbsp. unsalted butter

3 large onions, sliced

1 large shallot, finely chopped

1 garlic clove, minced

sea salt to taste

freshly ground black pepper to taste

¼ cup cooking wine

1 Tbsp. white wine vinegar

2 sprigs parsley

1 sprig thyme

1 bay leaf

4 cups beef broth

2 bread slices, toasted

4 oz. Gruyére cheese

Directions

1. Heat the butter in a large heavy pot over medium-high heat. Add the onions, shallots, and garlic and season with salt and pepper. Cook, stirring occasionally, until softened and dark brown, for 60–70 minutes.

2. Add the cooking wine and the vinegar. Bring to a boil, reduce the heat, and simmer until slightly reduced, about 3 minutes.

3. Tie the parsley, thyme, and bay leaf with kitchen twine; add to the pot along with the broth. Bring to a boil.

4. Reduce the heat, and simmer, stirring occasionally, until reduced to about 4 cups, for 35–40 minutes. Discard the herb bundle.

5. Preheat the oven to 450 degrees.

6. Place oven-proof bowls on a large rimmed baking sheet. Divide the soup among the bowls and top with the toasted bread and cheese. Bake for 6–8 minutes, until the cheese is bubbling and golden brown.

Romantic Tip:

People say marriage is 50-50. What if both of you gave 100-100? Try giving 100% today. Remind yourself throughout the day to give it your all. Then watch how it affects your relationship.

HOT AND SOUR SOUP

Whenever my husband and I go out to Asian restaurants, we both order the Hot and Sour soup. I love it, but I eat around the tofu. I am not a tofu eater. If you like tofu, you can add some to this soup to make it more traditional.

Ingredients

4 cups chicken broth

1 tsp garlic, minced

2 Tbsp. soy sauce

½ cup sweet onion, diced

1 Tbsp. fresh ginger, minced

7 oz. sliced mushrooms

1 Tbsp. agave nectar

1 Tbsp. red chili paste

¼ tsp. white pepper

4 Tbsp. rice vinegar

8 oz. sliced bamboo shoots, drained

8 oz. sliced water chestnuts, drained

2 Tbsp. cornstarch

2 Tbsp. water

1 egg slightly beaten

½ tsp. sesame oil

1 green onion, sliced

Directions

1. Bring the stock to a boil in a medium-large saucepan. Add the next seven ingredients (through the chili paste) and reduce the heat to simmer for 10 minutes.

2. Add the white pepper, rice vinegar, bamboo shoots, and water chestnuts; simmer for 10 minutes.

3. Mix the cornstarch with the water and slowly drizzle the slurry into the soup while stirring.

4. Bring the soup back up to a simmer and drizzle the eggs in a very thin stream over the surface of soup while stirring. Add the sesame oil.

5. Let the soup marinate at room temperature for 30 minutes, then reheat and serve garnished with sliced green onions.

Romantic Tip:

Send a love email every single day.

Christi Silbaugh

LOBSTER BISQUE

Using a crock-pot for this soup allows the rich lobster flavor to simmer for hours, while you go about your day.

Ingredients

1 shallot, minced

1 garlic clove, minced

1 (14.5-oz.) petite diced tomatoes with juice

16 oz. chicken broth

½ Tbsp. old bay seasoning

½ tsp. dill

¼ cup fresh parsley, chopped

½ tsp freshly ground black pepper

½ tsp. paprika

2 lobster tails

1 cup heavy whipping cream

Directions

1. Put the minced shallot and garlic in a small skillet with the olive oil until the shallot is wilted and starts to turn translucent.

2. Continue adding the tomatoes, chicken broth, old bay seasoning, dill, parsley, pepper, and paprika to the crock-pot.

3. With a sharp knife, cut off the fan part of the very end of the lobsters and add those to the crock-pot.

4. Stir, cover, and cook on low for 6 hours, or for 3 hours on high.

5. Take out the lobster shells and discard.

6. Using a blender or immersion blender, puree the soup mixture to your desired chunkiness. Add the soup back into the crock-pot if you used a regular blender.

7. Add your lobster tails to the soup, cover, and cook for 45 minutes on low, or until the shells turn red and the lobster meat is cooked.

8. Remove the lobster tails from the soup and let them cool slightly. While the lobster is cooling, add the cream and stir.

9. With a sharp knife, cut each lobster tail in half longways and remove the lobster flesh from the shells. Discard the shells and roughly chop the lobster meat and add it back into the soup. Serve immediately.

Christi Silbaugh

NAVY BEAN SOUP

A hearty soup that will warm you on a cold night.

Ingredients

¾ cups dried navy beans

2 carrots, peeled and thinly sliced

2 celery stalks, diced

½ sweet onion, diced

2 chicken bouillon cubes, crumbled

¾ tsp. onion powder

½ tsp. sea salt

½ tsp. dried parsley

½ tsp. dried basil

½ tsp. garlic powder

1 bay leaf

¼ tsp. pepper

4 cups chicken broth

optional:

Some people like ham or bacon in their navy bean soup. If you like that, you can add a cup or two of cooked ham or bacon.

Directions

1. Soak your navy beans in 8 cups of water overnight. Drain. Or used canned beans as an alternative.

2. In a slow cooker, combine all the ingredients and stir to blend.

3. Cover and cook on low for 9–10 hours, or until the beans are tender.

4. Discard the bay leaf and serve.

 Romantic Tip:

I love getting anything in writing from my man. He is not much of a writer, so when he takes the time to write for me, I feel extra special. I think everyone should take the time each day to write a little affirmation to their loved one. Make it loving. Tell them how much they mean to you. It keeps the spark alive until you are back in each other's arms.

RAMEN BOWL

This is not your typical college ramen! It is carefully made and full of yummy veggies and meat and a rich broth.

Ingredients

2 Tbsp. sesame oil

½ lb. boneless pork tenderloin, sliced into ⅓-inch pieces

8 dried red chili peppers

1 sweet onion, finely chopped

1 carrot, finely chopped

2 garlic cloves, crushed

1 inch piece ginger root, peeled and sliced

4 cups chicken broth

2 Tbsp. soy sauce

6 oz. Shiitake mushrooms, sliced

½ tsp. sea salt

1 pinch freshly ground black pepper

6 oz. ramen noodles

2 sheets nori seaweed sheets, sliced into bite-sized pieces

8 oz. bamboo shoots, sliced lengthwise

1 hard-boiled egg, sliced in half

2 green onion, sliced

Directions

1. Heat a stockpot over medium heat. Add the sesame oil and pork slices. Cook the pork until cooked through and set aside.

2. In the same pot, add the peppers and onion. Sweat them slightly.

3. Add the carrots, crushed garlic, and ginger. Cook for another 2–3 minutes.

4. Next, stir in the chicken broth, soy sauce, and mushrooms, and season with salt and pepper. Bring to a simmer and cook for 15–20 minutes.

5. Sieve the broth: Place a sieve over another saucepan and strain the broth. Then put it back on the heat.

6. Slice your pork into strips. Add the noodles, nori, and bamboo shoots to the broth and raise the heat to a simmer. Leave them to cook for about 3 minutes.

7. Place the noodles into two soup bowls and ladle the broth on top. Add the sliced hardboiled egg, the pork, and finally the green onions. Season with salt and pepper. Add a little more broth and your ramen is ready.

 Romantic Tip:
Get fancy by dressing up and splurging time on a loved one. It's a timeless way to tell someone you love them.

Christi Silbaugh

SPLIT PEA SOUP

A simple split pea soup recipe, hearty for a winter day. Easy to make and tasty!

Ingredients

⅛ cup olive oil

½ cup diced sweet onion

1 cup diced carrots

½ cup chopped celery

½ Tbsp. chopped garlic

4 cups chicken broth

1 (8-oz.) bag green split peas

1 bay leaf

sea salt to taste

freshly ground black pepper to taste

ham bone for cooking (optional)

Directions

1. Pour the olive oil into a large stockpot. Add the diced onion, carrots, celery, and garlic and cook for 3 minutes, stirring often.

2. Add the chicken broth, green split peas, and bay leaves. If you want to use a hambone to increase the flavor and add ham bits to your soup, add it here. Bring the soup to a boil. Reduce heat, cover, and simmer for 2 hours.

3. Stir well to break up the peas, and add salt and pepper to taste. Top with your favorite fresh herbs to garnish.

Romantic Tip:

Go on a date to your local comedy club for some laughs. Laughter really is the best medicine.

VEGETABLE SOUP

A bowl of all things wholesome. The perfect soup for a rainy day, or for cold and flu season.

Ingredients

1 quart vegetable broth

1 cup mushrooms, sliced

½ cup carrots, peeled, sliced

½ sweet onion, diced

½ Tbsp. freshly ground black pepper

½ Tbsp. basil

1 garlic clove, minced

1 tsp. thyme

1 bay leaf

sea salt to taste

freshly ground black pepper to taste

1 cup potatoes, peeled and cut into 1-in. bites

Directions

1. Mix all the ingredients except the potatoes together in a crock-pot, and cook on high for 3 hours.

2. Add the potatoes and cook another 30 minutes. Serve hot.

Romantic Tip:

Go on a camping trip together. It doesn't cost much. There are no TVs, computers, or other distractions.

Christi Silbaugh

VEGETARIAN CHILI

Break out your soup pot and fix up a batch of this delicious, spicy vegetarian chili today! It's ready in no time, and is packed with vegetables, beans, and flavor.

Ingredients

½ sweet onion, finely chopped

2 garlic cloves, chopped

2 jalapeño, stemmed, seeded, and finely diced

1 bell pepper, chopped

1 celery stalk, finely diced

½ tsp. oregano

½ Tbsp. ground cumin

2 Tbsp. chili powder

½ tsp. cayenne pepper

1 tsp. salt

½ tsp. black pepper

1 (15-oz.) can kidney beans

1 (15-oz.) can black beans

1 (7.5-oz.) can tomato sauce

1 (15-oz.) can tomato puree

Directions

1. In a large stock pot, add the onion, garlic, jalapeño, bell pepper, and celery and mix together.

2. Add the rest of the ingredients and bring the soup to a boil. Then reduce the heat and let it simmer for at least one hour.

3. Serve hot.

Romantic Tip:

Take a hard look in the mirror. See how you can turn it around and be a giver for your spouse, even if it means getting nothing in return. Try to do at least one unselfish deed for others each day. It will change your life and your relationships.

Christi Silbaugh

MAIN DISHES

20 Clove Garlic Chicken

Asian Fish Sliders

Asian-Inspired Grilled
Flat Steak

Avocado Enchiladas

Bacon Wrapped
Macaroni and Cheese

Bacon Wrapped Scallops

Baked Omelettes

Beef Wellington

Blackened Salmon

Blue Cheese Burgers

Breakfast Skillet

Breakfast Tacos

Chicken Cordon Bleu

Chicken Milanese

Chicken Parmesan

Chicken Saltimbocca

Chilean Sea Bass with
Green Gazpacho

Chimichangas

Crispy Snapper with
Spicy Basil Sauce

Crock-Pot Beef Roast

Fillet Mignon with
Mushroom Sauce

Fish Tacos

Halibut Gribiche

Herb-Crusted Salmon

Lasagna Bolognese

Lasagna Cups

Lemon Dill Shrimp and Corn

Negimaki

Orange Chicken

Overnight Steel-Cut Oats

Parmesan Dill Sea Bass

Pork Tamales

Scallops with Beurre Blanc
over Orzo

Shepherd's Pie

Spicy Red Snapper
over Lemon Rice

Sriracha Salmon

Sticky Garlic Chicken

Thai Coconut Lemon
Lime Shrimp

Thai Red Curry Chicken

White Enchiladas

20 CLOVE GARLIC CHICKEN

This 20 clove garlic chicken has been a favorite of ours for years. It is a deceivingly light dish that turns out perfect every single time.

Ingredients

1 boneless and skinless chicken breast, cut in half

⅛ tsp. sea salt

⅛ tsp. freshly ground black pepper

½ Tbsp. canola oil (or other low saturated fat oil)

20 garlic cloves, unpeeled

¼ cup white cooking wine

½ cup chicken broth

½ Tbsp. lemon juice

½ tsp. dried basil

¼ tsp. oregano

2 tsp. corn starch

2 Tbsp. chicken broth

Directions

1. Rinse the chicken and pat it dry. Season with salt and pepper.

2. In a skillet, heat the oil over medium-high heat. Add the chicken and garlic cloves.

3. Cook the chicken for 2–3 minutes on each side or just until brown, turning once. Slowly add the cooking wine, broth, lemon juice, basil, and oregano.

4. Simmer covered for 6–8 minutes or until the chicken is tender. Use a slotted spoon to transfer the chicken and garlic to a warm serving platter; keep warm.

5. In a small bowl or cup, mix together the corn starch and the 2 tablespoons broth and stir it into the pan juices. Bring the sauce to boiling, then pour it over the chicken and serve. I serve it over rice or quinoa with a side of garlic green beans.

Romantic Tip:

Make note of something your partner likes when window shopping, and pick it up for him or her. Leave it as a surprise, for no reason at all, somewhere he or she will be sure to find it.

Christi Silbaugh

ASIAN FISH SLIDERS

This is my answer to avoiding fast food and restaurant fried fish sandwiches. It gives you all the great flavor, without the high processed ingredients.

Ingredients

for the breading:

1 cup panko breadcrumbs

½ tsp. ground ginger

½ tsp. sea salt

¼ tsp. paprika

⅛ tsp. pepper

½ lb. fish fillets (any white fish will work)

2 Tbsp. butter

1 Tbsp. olive oil

for the flour dredge:

¼ cup flour

½ tsp. salt

¼ tsp. pepper

2 eggs

for the cabbage slaw:

1 cup shredded cabbage

1½ Tbsp. rice wine vinegar

1 Tbsp. soy sauce

1 Tbsp. peanut oil

¼ Tbsp. sesame oil

¼ Tbsp. honey

¼ Tbsp. lime juice

1 pinch cayenne pepper

1 pinch red pepper flakes

1 pinch sea salt

1 pinch pepper

for the yogurt sauce:

¼ cup kefir cheese (spreadable Greek yogurt)

1 Tbsp. dill pickle juice

½ tsp. ground ginger

¼ tsp. hot sauce

6 dinner rolls of your choice

Directions

1. Toss the panko crumbs with ginger, salt, paprika, and pepper.

2. Cut the fish fillets to fit on your dinner rolls.

3. Prepare a dipping station. Have one bowl ready with the flour dredge mixed together. Whip the eggs in another bowl. Set out one larger bowl with the breading.

4. Start by dipping your fish in the flour to coat on each side.

5. Next dip the fish in the eggs.

6. Last, coat the fish in the breading mixture.

7. Melt 2 tablespoons butter and 1 tablespoon olive oil in a skillet and add the fish. Cook each side until browned, turning once.

8. Meanwhile, prepare the sauce. Mix together all the yogurt sauce ingredients in a small bowl and set aside. Prepare cabbage slaw.

9. When the fish is almost done, prepare your buns. Spread each bun with the yogurt sauce mixture. Place cabbage slaw on each bun. Top with the fish fillet.

10. Dab a little more of the sauce on the top bun and top the fish. Use a toothpick or mini skewer to hold the sandwiches together while serving.

Romantic Tip:

At night, lay a blanket on the grass and star gaze together. Make a wish on a shooting star.

ASIAN-INSPIRED GRILLED FLAT STEAK

This recipe is perfect for a work day. Marinate it before you go to work and cook it up in less than 10 minutes when you get home.

Ingredients

¼ cup soy sauce

¼ cup cooking sherry

⅛ cup honey

1 Tbsp. sesame oil

2 Tbsp. minced ginger

1 Tbsp. minced garlic

½ tsp. crushed red pepper flakes

1 lb. thin sliced sirloin steak

roasted sesame seeds

green onions for garnish

Directions

1. Add all the ingredients except the steak, seeds, and green onions, and whisk them together in a bowl.

2. Place the steaks in a ziploc bag. Marinate and chill in the refrigerator for 3–10 hours.

3. Grill the steaks on high heat for 2 minutes on each side for medium rare steaks, longer for well-done. Allow the steaks to rest for 5 minutes before slicing and serving.

4. Sprinkle roasted sesame seeds and green onion slivers on top to garnish.

Romantic Tip:

Never put yourself down. Criticizing and putting yourself down in front of your loved one is a way of insulting his taste. Realize that if they are with you, it's because they chose you and want to be with you.

Main Dishes

AVOCADO ENCHILADAS

While this dish looks and tastes sinful, the avocado cream topping really makes these healthy, organic, free range enchiladas. With high fiber, healthy fats, cholesterol lowering properties, blood pressure controlling nutrients, and so much more, avocados should be a daily staple.

Ingredients

1 Tbsp. olive oil

½ lb. chicken breasts

½ tsp. chili powder

½ tsp. cumin

½ tsp. paprika

½ tsp. sea salt

¼ cup chicken broth

6 organic corn tortillas

½ cup Monterey Jack cheese

⅛ cup chopped cilantro

salsa

for the avocado cream:

2 large ripe avocados, preferably haas, pitted and roughly chopped

½ serrano pepper

¼ cup plain Greek yogurt

2 Tbsp. fresh squeezed lime juice

¼ cup roughly chopped cilantro

¼ tsp. sea salt

⅛ cup water

Directions

1. Preheat the oven to 350 degrees.

2. In a large ovenproof skillet, add the olive oil and bring it to medium-high heat. Season the chicken breasts with the chili powder, cumin, paprika, and sea salt.

3. Add the chicken to the skillet and brown it on each side, leaving the middle uncooked. Add the chicken broth. Place the skillet in the oven and cook for 10 minutes.

4. While the chicken is cooking, make your avocado cream. Add all the ingredients to your food processor. Pulse several times until a chunky cream is formed.

5. In a small baking dish, spread some of the avocado cream in the bottom. This will keep the enchiladas from sticking.

6. Pull the chicken out of the oven and shred it into small pieces. It should fall apart easily. I use two forks to pull it apart.

7. Steam or heat your tortillas to soften them. I use a steamer because I don't like added calories from oil.

8. Place approximately 2 tablespoons of chicken and 1 teaspoon cheese into each corn tortilla. Roll closed and place in the baking dish seam-side down. Top with the remaining avocado cream and cheese. Place in the oven for 20 minutes. Top with cilantro and salsa.

Christi Silbaugh

BACON WRAPPED MACARONI AND CHEESE

The saying "Everything is better with bacon" definitely applies to this scrumptious macaroni and cheese.

Ingredients

½ pkg. bacon

1 Tbsp. butter

½ Tbsp. flour

½ cup whole milk

1 tsp. minced garlic

2 oz. sharp cheddar cheese, grated

2 oz. smoked Gouda cheese, grated

1 egg

2 cups cooked elbow macaroni

salt and black pepper to taste

Parmesan cheese, freshly grated

Romantic Tip:

Do something special for your love for no reason. Don't wait for a birthday or anniversary. Those are just days when you are expected to do something. Let them know their love is important to you every day, not just on holidays.

Directions

1. Preheat the oven to 400 degrees. Lightly mist a muffin tin with cooking spray and set aside.

2. To make the muffins, start with the bacon. Cook it on a griddle until just before it would get crispy. Drain the bacon; then, working quickly, wrap the bacon around the inside of each muffin tin.

3. In a small sauce pot, melt the butter over medium heat.

4. Add the flour, mixing it into the butter until thick. Stir in the milk and garlic and raise the temperature to bring the mixture to just under a boil. Add the cheese and whisk the mixture together until thoroughly combined into a cheese sauce.

5. Remove the cheese sauce from the heat, then mix in the egg until combined. This will bind the macaroni together.

6. In a large bowl, combine the pasta, cheese sauce, salt, and pepper and mix together. Spoon the mixture evenly into the bacon-lined cups of your muffin tin.

7. Sprinkle with Parmesan cheese. Bake for 10–15 minutes, until the tops are slightly brown. Let cool 5 minutes before removing the macaroni from the muffin tin.

BACON WRAPPED SCALLOPS

Since the American way of thinking is that "everything is better with bacon," you can imagine my husband's delight for these babies. They look so fancy, like they took you hours to make. Let your guests think that. They are actually very simple to make. Bring these to dinner and impress your guests!

Ingredients

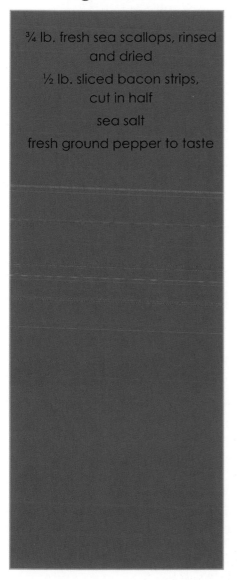

¾ lb. fresh sea scallops, rinsed and dried

½ lb. sliced bacon strips, cut in half

sea salt

fresh ground pepper to taste

Directions

1. Preheat your oven broiler. Spray a rimmed baking sheet with non-stick spray.

2. Wrap each scallop with a piece of bacon and secure with a toothpick.

3. Place the bacon-wrapped scallops onto the prepared baking dish and season them with salt and pepper. Cook them under the broiler on high for about 20 minutes, or until the bacon is cooked through and the top is brown.

4. Serve alone or over fresh pasta.

 Romantic Tip:
Don't forget to say "thank you" when your love does little things for you.

Main Dishes

BAKED OMELETTES

You can prepare these the night before, keep them in the fridge, and just pop them in the oven in the morning for a fast, easy, and scrumptious breakfast.

Ingredients

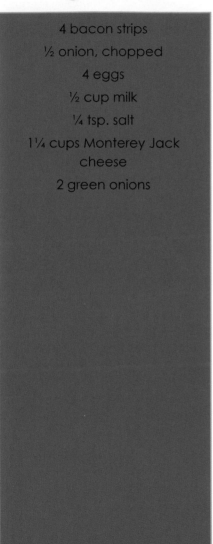

4 bacon strips

½ onion, chopped

4 eggs

½ cup milk

¼ tsp. salt

1¼ cups Monterey Jack cheese

2 green onions

Directions

1. Preheat the oven to 350 degrees.

2. Cook the bacon until crisp. Drain the pan, but don't clean the pan. Set the bacon aside.

3. In the same pan, sauté the onion until tender and set aside.

4. In a large bowl, beat the eggs. Add the milk, salt, 1 cup cheese, bacon, and sautéed onions. Transfer the mixture to a greased, shallow 2-quart baking dish, or to two individual baking dishes. Top with the sliced green onions.

5. Bake uncovered at 350 degrees for 30 minutes.

6. Take the omelettes out of the oven and sprinkle them with the remaining cheese. Bake for another 10 minutes. Serve warm.

Romantic Tip:

Sometimes life is just hectic and there isn't much time for anything but household duties and work. When time allows, do your partner's household chores as well as your own. Then, when you're both home for the night, ditch the chores and do something fun instead. Everyone deserves a break, and this time it's your love's turn.

Christi Silbaugh

BEEF WELLINGTON

Don't be scared to tackle this dish. I was so pleased with how simple it was to make. This is a dish that is very easily made ahead, with results that will definitely wow your mate.

Ingredients

1 Tbsp. olive oil

2 (8-oz.) fillet mignon

salt and pepper to taste

Dijon mustard

5 oz. crimini mushrooms

1 Tbsp. butter

1 sprig of fresh thyme

2 oz. apple cider vinegar

6 slices prosciutto, thinly sliced

½ lb. puff pastry, thawed if frozen

a little flour for dusting

2 egg yolks

1 tsp. water

Directions

1. Heat the olive oil in a large pan on high heat. Season the fillet generously with salt and pepper. Sear the fillet in the pan on all sides, until well browned.

2. Remove the fillet from the pan, then brush the fillet on all sides with the Dijon mustard. Set aside.

3. Chop the mushrooms finely in a food processor. Heat a large sauté pan on medium-high heat. Add the butter, thyme, and apple cider vinegar to the chopped mushrooms into the pan and let them cook down.

4. When the moisture has boiled away, set the mushroom mixture aside to cool.

5. Roll out a large piece of plastic wrap. Lay out the slices of prosciutto on the plastic wrap so that they overlap. Spread the mushroom mixture over the prosciutto. Place the beef fillet in the middle, then roll the mushroom and prosciutto over the fillet, using the plastic wrap so that you do this tightly.

6. Wrap the beef fillet into a tight barrel shape, twisting the ends of the plastic wrap to secure. Refrigerate for at least 20 minutes.

 Romantic Tip:

When your partner raves about a dish, surprise them with a homemade version of it without letting them know. You'll be sure to make them smile!

7. Preheat the oven to 400 degrees. On a lightly floured surface, roll out the puff pastry sheet to a size that will wrap around the beef fillet. Unwrap the fillet from the plastic wrap and place it in the middle of the pastry dough.

8. Brush the edges of the pastry with the beaten eggs. Fold the pastry around the fillet, cutting off any excess at the ends. (Pastry that is more than 2 layers thick will not cook all the way; try to limit the overlap.) Place on a small plate, seam side down, and brush the beaten egg yolks all over the top. Chill for 5–10 minutes.

9. Place the pastry-wrapped fillet on a baking pan. Brush the exposed surface again with beaten eggs. Score the top of the pastry with a sharp knife. Sprinkle the top with coarse salt. Bake for 25–35 minutes. The pastry should be nicely golden when done. (To ensure that your roast is medium rare, test with an instant read meat thermometer. Pull out at 125–130°F for medium rare.)

10. Remove from the oven and let rest for 10 minutes before slicing.

BLACKENED SALMON

This meal is perfect for those nights when you need to get dinner on in less than 30 minutes. It's really one of the tastiest things I have ever put in my mouth. Plus, it's naturally gluten-free.

Ingredients

1 tsp. garlic salt

½ tsp. paprika

½ tsp. onion powder

½ tsp. oregano

½ tsp. black pepper

¼ tsp. cayenne pepper

¼ tsp. thyme

1 lb. wild caught salmon, cut into two 8 oz. fillets

Directions

1. Combine the garlic salt, paprika, onion powder, oregano, black pepper, cayenne pepper, and thyme in a small bowl and mix to combine.

2. Rub the mixture on both sides of the two fish fillets.

3. Heat a large cast iron skillet over medium-high heat. Spray the skillet with non-stick cooking spray and add the fish.

4. Cook for 5–8 minutes on each side, or until the fish flakes easily with a fork.

Romantic Tip:

Spend a few minutes daydreaming about your love and the romantic things you want to do together.

BLUE CHEESE BURGERS

You can easily modify this recipe and use any of your favorite cheeses. My husband's favorite is blue cheese, and this is his favorite burger.

Ingredients

1 Tbsp. olive oil

8 oz. sliced mushrooms

½ red onion, thinly sliced

¾ lb. ground beef

½ Tbsp. onion powder

1 Tbsp. Worcestershire sauce

½ tsp. sea salt

½ tsp. freshly ground black pepper

4 oz. blue cheese

½ tsp. salt

2 large hamburger buns, toasted

Romantic Tip:

Leave a romantic note or photo somewhere your partner will find it. You'll be sure to make their day!

Directions

1. Heat the olive oil in a large, heavy-bottomed saucepan on medium heat. Add the mushrooms and the ½ teaspoon sea salt and stir briefly to coat with oil. Cook without stirring for 5 minutes. Add the onions.

2. Stir and cook for another 5 minutes. Flip the mixture so that the onions on the bottom of the pot are now on top, and cook for another 5 minutes. Flip one more time, lower the heat, and allow the onions to caramelize while you finish the burgers.

3. In a large bowl, mix the ground beef, onion powder, Worcestershire, salt, and pepper until just combined. Do not overmix or your patties will be tough.

4. Divide into two portions and form patties, but don't press too hard. The patties should be uniform in thickness. Smooth out any cracks with your fingers.

5. Preheat a cast-iron skillet to high heat and add the burger patties. Cook for about 2 minutes and then flip. Add enough blue cheese to cover the patties completely, cover with a lid, and cook for another 2–3 minutes for medium to medium rare burgers.

6. Remove the patties carefully using a metal spatula, and transfer to the toasted buns. Top with the caramelized mushrooms and onions, your favorite lettuce or greens (I love baby spinach on these).

Christi Silbaugh

BREAKFAST SKILLET

I have mini 6-inch cast iron skillets that makes this very convenient to serve. You can whip up a loaded breakfast skillet in under 15 minutes. Any or all of the ingredients are optional. If you don't like bacon, skip it or use sausage. The possibilities are endless, and it is easy to make everyone happy with their personalized skillet breakfast.

Ingredients

4 strips of bacon

4 Tbsp. butter

½ cup chopped onion

1 cup coarsely chopped mushrooms

1 jalapeño chile, stemmed, seeded and finely diced

1 cup cooked hash browns

4 eggs

Directions

1. Cook your bacon slices and set aside.

2. Melt the butter in a skillet and add the onion, mushrooms, and jalapeño. Cook them until they begin to brown.

3. Stir in the cooked hash browns and top with bacon.

4. Fry the eggs, or cook them however you'd like. Add them to the top of your skillet and serve.

Romantic Tip:

Spend some time together at a local pastry shop. Then take a long walk, hand in hand, with that extra boost you just got.

Main Dishes

BREAKFAST TACOS

If you like things spicy, chorizo is the way to go. If you would like a milder flavor, you can use the sausage of your choice.

Ingredients

1 tsp. vegetable oil

¼ cup finely chopped sweet onion

4 oz. chorizo sausage

2 Tbsp. stemmed, seeded and finely diced jalapeño chile

4 eggs

8 organic corn tortillas

⅓ cup pepper-jack cheese, grated

green onions for garnish (optional)

Directions

1. In a large skillet add the oil, sweet onion, chorizo sausage, and jalapeño. Cook on medium heat for about 5 minutes, until the sausage is cooked through.

2. Crack the eggs in a bowl and whisk.

3. After the sausage is cooked through, scrape it to one side and pour the eggs into the other side. Cook until the eggs are cooked through, then stir them together with the sausage.

4. Heat the tortillas in a tortilla warmer (if you don't have a tortilla warmer, wrap your tortillas securely with parchment paper). Cook on high for 2 minutes in the microwave oven.

5. To assemble, lay 2 corn tortillas on a plate, then add your chorizo/egg mixture and top with the pepper-jack cheese. Repeat with the remaining ingredients.

6. Top with green onions and serve!

Romantic Tip:

Take your love dancing and ask the DJ to dedicate a slow romantic song to your love, from you. Then dance the night away.

Christi Silbaugh

CHICKEN CORDON BLEU

This may not be the healthiest way to eat chicken, but it sure is the tastiest! The pan sauce makes this dish extraordinary.

Ingredients

1 boneless and skinless chicken breast, cut in half

2 slices fontina cheese

2 slices ham

½ Tbsp. flour

1 Tbsp. Parmesan cheese freshly grated

½ tsp. paprika

3 Tbsp. butter

½ cup dry white wine

½ tsp. chicken bouillon granules

½ Tbsp. corn starch

½ cup heavy whipping cream

Romantic Tip:
Each of you make a romantic bucket list to share during an upcoming romantic evening. Make a plan to fulfill one of the fantasies on the list within one week.

Directions

1. Pound the chicken breast halves as thin as you can with a tenderizer.

2. Place a cheese and ham slice together. Fold the ham over the cheese to help keep the cheese from oozing out once it has melted. Place on each flattened chicken breast. Fold the edges of the chicken over the filling and secure with toothpicks.

3. Mix the flour, Parmesan, and paprika in a small bowl, then coat the chicken pieces.

4. Heat the butter in a large skillet over medium-high heat and cook the chicken until browned on all sides.

5. Add the wine and bouillon. Reduce the heat to low, cover, and simmer for 20 minutes, until the chicken is no longer pink and the juices run clear.

6. Remove the toothpicks and transfer the chicken breasts to a warm platter. Blend the cornstarch with the cream in a small bowl and whisk slowly into the skillet. Cook, stirring until thickened.

7. Pour over the chicken. Serve warm. I serve mine over a bed of baby spinach and it is scrumptious!

Christi Silbaugh

CHICKEN MILANESE

I love a good Milanese sauce. The lemon cream complements this chicken so nicely. This is right up there with my all-time favorite chicken dishes.

Ingredients

1½ Tbsp. unsalted butter, cut into small pieces

1 shallot, minced

¼ cup heavy whipping cream

¼ cup white wine vinegar

1 tsp. agave nectar

¼ cup chicken stock

½ Tbsp. chopped fresh sage

1 tsp. lemon juice

1 dash cayenne pepper

sea salt

freshly ground black pepper

½ cup seasoned bread crumbs

⅛ cup Parmesan cheese

1 tsp. lemon zest

½ tsp. dried thyme

1 egg

1 chicken breast, cut in half

canola oil (or other low saturated fat oil) for frying

⅛ cup chopped fresh parsley, plus extra for garnish

lemon for garnish (optional)

Directions

1. In a medium pot over medium heat, melt 1 tablespoon of the butter. Add the shallots and cook until softened, about 4 minutes.

2. Add the cream, wine vinegar, agave, and stock. Bring this mixture to a boil. Simmer until the mixture is reduced by half. This can take anywhere from 10–20 minutes.

3. Remove the pot from the heat. Whisk in the remaining butter, 1 tablespoon at a time, stirring well between each addition.

4. Add the sage, lemon, cayenne, and parsley, and salt and pepper to taste. Cover and set aside.

5. Mix the bread crumbs, cheese, lemon zest, and thyme. Transfer to a plate.

6. Beat the egg and season with salt and pepper. Transfer to a shallow bowl.

Romantic Tip:

Surprise your partner with lunch at their job. Sync up your lunch time with your love's, make them their favorite lunch, and take it to their office. If you're not able to stay to enjoy it with them, leave it with a sweet note that makes them smile from ear to ear.

Christi Silbaugh

7. Hammer your chicken breast pieces until they are thin chicken cutlets. Season the chicken cutlets with salt and pepper on both sides.

8. Dip 1 cutlet in the egg mixture and remove, letting the excess drip back in the bowl. Lay the cutlet in the crumb mixture and, with dry hands, toss the crumbs over the top to coat the chicken. Repeat with the remaining cutlets.

9. Fill a large skillet with ¼ inch of oil. Heat over medium heat (350–375 is ideal) until the oil shimmers.

10. Add the two breaded cutlets to the pan. Cook for 3 minutes on each side, or until they are a dark golden brown.

11. Lower the heat to medium and cook for another 4 minutes, turning once. The cutlets should be brown and crisp.

12. Lay the cutlets on prepared paper towels to drain.

13. Serve cutlets with sauce, and optional lemon and parsley for garnish.

CHICKEN PARMESAN

A classic Italian dish prepared with tomato sauce and mozzarella that will leave your taste buds dancing.

Ingredients

1 (8-oz.) pkg. spaghetti noodles

1 chicken breast

salt and pepper to taste

¼ cup flour

2 eggs, beaten

½ cup bread crumbs

½ cup finely grated Parmesan cheese

1 tsp. Italian seasoning

canola oil for frying

1 cup marinara sauce

½ cup shredded mozzarella cheese

Romantic Tip:
Buy a tree and invite your partner to plant it with you. Explain that this tree represents the love between you both that will grow over the years.

Directions

1. Preheat your oven to 350 degrees and prepare the spaghetti according to the package directions.

2. Trim the fat off the chicken breast and rinse it off. Cut it up into 4 pieces. Salt and pepper your trimmed chicken breast pieces.

3. Line up a dipping station. Put the flour in one bowl, the eggs in another, and the crumbs, cheese, and Italian seasoning in another bowl.

4. Start by generously covering the chicken with flour.

5. Next, dip the chicken in the beaten eggs, and then into the crumb/cheese mixture.

6. Set the chicken aside while you preheat your skillet.

7. Heat a skillet over medium-high heat and add the canola oil. Heat to 350 degrees.

8. Add the chicken in small batches. Cook for about 5 minutes per side.

9. Place the chicken in a baking dish. Top the chicken with marinara, followed by the shredded mozzarella.

10. Bake for 15 minutes and serve immediately over the cooked spaghetti.

Christi Silbaugh

CHICKEN SALTIMBOCCA

Saltimbocca means "jump into the mouth" in Italian. You will see why this dish is named after that phrase as soon as you make it!

Ingredients

1 boneless, skinless chicken breast

¼ cup flour

¼ tsp. sea salt

⅛ tsp. freshly ground black pepper

3 Tbsp. olive oil, divided

8 oz. sliced mushrooms

6 oz. sweet marsala or sweet cooking wine

6 oz. chicken stock

1 pinch ground sage

1 pinch freshly ground black pepper

1 Tbsp. heavy whipping cream

2 Tbsp. unsalted butter

2 Tbsp. flour

2 slices prosciutto

3 oz. fontina cheese

olive oil

6 oz. baby spinach

Directions

1. Cut the chicken breast into two pieces. Pound the chicken breasts with the flat side of a meat hammer and cut into serving size pieces.

2. In a large ziploc bag, mix the flour, salt, and pepper. Add the chicken and shake until it is fully covered.

3. Place the floured breasts in a large sauté pan with 2 tablespoons of the olive oil and sauté. Cook the chicken for 5 minutes on each side and remove from the pan.

4. Add 1 tablespoon olive oil to the pan, add in the sliced mushrooms, and sauté until soft.

5. Add all but 2 ounces of the marsala or cooking wine to pan to deglaze and allow it to cook for a minute. Then add the chicken stock, sage, and black pepper, and place the chicken breasts back into the pan.

 Romantic Tip:

In this digital age, it is so easy to snap pictures all time and view them on social media, without having any hard copies. I think it is important to have hard copies of your favorite memories. There is something romantic about spending time looking through books together that are filled with your own memories. Print your favorites off and go through them together.

Christi Silbaugh

6. Reduce the heat and continue to cook while the sauce is reducing. Once the sauce has started to reduce, add the cream and mix well.

7. Take the butter and coat it in flour, then add it to the sauce. As the sauce begins to thicken, remove it from the heat.

8. Place the chicken breast in a baking dish and top it with a slice of proscuitto and slices of fontina cheese. Place it in a 350 degree oven for about 15 minutes, or until the cheese has melted. In another sauté pan, add in a little olive oil and the baby spinach, sauté until completely cooked, and set aside (make sure you drain off any extra oil).

9. Three minutes before the chicken breasts are done, start to slowly reheat the marsala sauce and spinach. Add the remaining marsala.

10. On a serving platter or individual plates, arrange the dish with the sautéed spinach, chicken breast, mushrooms. and marsala sauce in that order.

CHILEAN SEA BASS WITH GREEN GAZPACHO

You eat first with your eyes. The magnificent colors of this dish will make your taste buds anticipate the first bite. And they will not be disappointed!

Ingredients

½ large English cucumber, coarsely chopped

½ cup chopped green onion

1 jalapeño pepper, chopped

½ cup chopped fresh cilantro

2 garlic cloves, chopped

4 Tbsp. extra virgin olive oil

2 Tbsp. white vinegar

1 Tbsp. canola oil

sea salt

freshly ground black pepper

2 (6-8-oz.) chilean sea bass fillets

fresh slivers of jalapeño pepper for garnish (optional)

chopped tomatoes for garnish (optional

Romantic Tip:

Spruce up your wardrobe with some new romantic items that are sure to wow your partner.

Directions

1. Preheat your oven to 350 degrees.

2. Combine the cucumber, green onions, jalapeño, cilantro, garlic, olive oil, and vinegar in a food processor or blender. Pulse the machine to create the sauce, making sure not to overdo it—you do want some texture. Move the sauce to a bowl, then cover and chill until you are ready to use it.

3. Heat the canola oil in a large non-stick skillet (cast iron is best) over medium-high heat. Season both sides of each fish fillet with with sea salt and freshly ground pepper to taste. When it is hot, slip the fish into the skillet. Cook for 4 minutes on the first side, then carefully flip and cook for another 3 minutes.

4. Remove the skillet from the stove-top and put it in the preheated oven until the fillet is just opaque, but still very moist in the center, for about 10 minutes. If you are using a different style of fish, you may need to skip this step. Chilean sea bass is very thick and needs extra cooking time.

5. To serve, spoon some sauce into a shallow bowl, top with a piece of fish, and sprinkle with sliced peppers and fresh chopped tomatoes if desired.

Christi Silbaugh

CHIMICHANGAS

When you're in need of some comfort food, these will hit the spot! These have almost half the calories of a traditional deep fried Chimichangas, but they are just as crispy baked in the oven, because of the tiny little bit of brushed butter on top.

Ingredients

½ lb. ground beef

1 oz. taco seasoning (use a packet or make your own)

½ cup water

½ tsp. ground cumin

1 tsp. chopped fresh oregano

1 Tbsp. chopped fresh cilantro

1 Tbsp. stemmed, seeded, and finely diced jalapeño chile

¼ cup diced tomatoes

1 green onion, chopped

¼ cup sour cream

1 cup shredded cheddar cheese, divided

2 large flour tortillas

2 Tbsp. butter melted

optional garnishes:
tomatoes, lettuce, guacamole, salsa, sour cream, cheese, onions

Directions

1. Preheat the oven to 450 degrees.

2. Sauté the ground beef until it is cooked through and starting to brown. Add the taco seasoning and stir. Add the water and stir. Over medium-low heat, cook until the liquid has reduced to two-thirds.

3. Add the cumin, oregano, cilantro, jalapeño, tomatoes, and green onions. Simmer until the rest of the liquid has evaporated. Remove from the heat and let cool for 5 minutes. Stir in the sour cream and ½ cup of the cheddar cheese.

4. Lay the tortillas on wax paper and brush both sides with the melted butter. Spoon ½ of the filling into the center of each tortilla and fold like an envelope.

5. Put the tortillas seam-side down on a non-stick sheet pan, spaced so they do not touch. Bake for 20–25 minutes or until golden and crisp. Serve with your favorite garnishes.

Romantic Tip:

There is something powerful about the moonlight, especially along the water. Seeing the moon reflect off the water is peaceful and romantic. I highly recommend you get out there and experience it with your love. Make a plan to take a moonlit walk on the beach, bay, lake, or any other romantic place near your home.

Christi Silbaugh

CRISPY SNAPPER WITH SPICY BASIL SAUCE

The perfect combination of crispy, sweet, and spicy. If you aren't a big spice fan, you can always use bell peppers instead of Thai chile peppers.

Ingredients

2 (8-oz.) snapper fillets

¼ cup flour

1 egg

1 Tbsp. water

¾ cup panko breadcrumbs

4 Tbsp. canola oil, divided

6 shallots, minced

3 garlic cloves, minced

6 Thai chile peppers, diced

1 bell pepper, chopped

¼ cup chicken stock

¼ cup fish sauce

2 Tbsp. soy sauce

2 Tbsp. agave nectar

½ lime, juiced

1 tsp. cornstarch

1 tsp. cold water

1 cup Thai basil leaves

Directions

1. Pat dry the snapper fillets with a paper towel.

2. Set up a plate with flour, a bowl with the egg beaten with the water, and a plate with the panko breadcrumbs. Dredge each fillet in the flour, followed by the egg wash, then in the panko breadcrumbs, and set aside.

3. In a sauté pan or medium pot, heat 1 tablespoon of the canola oil over medium-high heat. Then sauté the shallots, garlic, chile peppers, and bell pepper until the shallots start to darken and the bell pepper is softened, for about 5 minutes.

4. Add the stock, fish sauce, soy sauce, agave, and lime juice, and stir together thoroughly. Bring to a boil and let simmer until slightly reduced, about 3–5 minutes.

 Romantic Tip:
Time. It's something that gets away from us so easily. We have to choose what we will accomplish and what we will let slide. Unfortunately, it is usually our relationships that we skimp on. I cannot stress enough the importance of putting our relationships first. Take time away from the computer, smart phone, and outside conflicts. Just put it all away. Focus on just the two of you.

Christi Silbaugh

5. Stir in the cornstarch and cold water and let simmer until thickened, about 1–2 minutes.

6. Stir in the Thai basil leaves and cook until fragrant, about 1–2 minutes. Lower the heat to the lowest setting to keep the sauce warm until ready to serve.

7. In a large sauté pan, heat 3 tablespoons of canola oil over high heat, and then add the coated fish fillets.

8. Cook the fish until the bottom is crispy and brown, about 3–5 minutes. Flip the fish and continue cooking for another 3–5 minutes, until the other side is crispy and brown, and the fish can be easily flaked with a fork. Move the fish to a plate lined with paper towels.

9. Serve the crispy fish fillets topped with the Thai basil sauce.

CROCK-POT BEEF ROAST

So easy, you can just throw it in a pot and enjoy your day. This recipe serves four.

Ingredients

½ Tbsp. garlic powder

½ Tbsp. onion powder

½ tsp. chili powder

½ Tbsp. salt

¼ Tbsp. pepper

¼ Tbsp. Italian seasoning

2–3 lb. beef tri-tip roast

1 Tbsp. canola oil (or other low saturated fat oil)

½ sweet onion, chopped into big chunks

3 garlic cloves, minced

½ cup peeled and chopped carrots

½ cup mushrooms

1 bay leaf

1 sprig thyme

¼ cup water

Directions

1. In a small bowl, mix together the garlic powder, onion powder, chili powder, salt, pepper, and Italian seasoning. Rub it all over your raw roast.

2. In a large pan, add the canola oil and heat up over medium-high heat. Sear your roast on all sides in the pan until it is golden brown, about 2 minutes per side. This will help retain the flavor while it roasts.

3. Add the seared meat to a large crock-pot. Top it with all your chopped vegetables and mushrooms, and pour in any remaining seasonings that are left in the pan or bowl. Add the water and top with the bay leaf and thyme.

4. Cover and cook on high for 3–4 hours, or on low for 6-8 hours. Adjust the seasoning with salt and pepper if needed.

 Romantic Tip:

In this day and age technology is everywhere. There is almost never a time when you aren't tweeting, facebooking, texting, skyping, or pinning. I have taken steps to turn the media off in the evening. We spend more time walking, playing games, and exploring. I really recommend you try some media-free time together. You might be surprised how much turning the media off turns your partner on.

Main Dishes

FILLET MIGNON WITH MUSHROOM SAUCE

Meat lovers will go nuts over this recipe of tender fillet mignon and succulent mushroom sauce.

Ingredients

2 (8-oz.) fillet mignon

coarse cracked black pepper

sea salt

splash of olive oil

2 shallots, minced

1 cup shiitake mushrooms

2 Tbsp. brandy

¾ cup chicken broth

1 Tbsp. butter

lemon juice

Directions

1. Bring the steaks to room temperature (this takes about 30 minutes).

2. Preheat the oven to 350 degrees.

3. When the steaks are at room temperature, start heating a cast iron skillet over medium-high heat. Generously salt and pepper both sides of the steaks and press the salt and pepper into the surface to ensure it sticks.

4. When the skillet is very hot, place the steaks in the pan and allow them to brown, undisturbed, until they don't stick to the pan anymore. Flip and brown them for another few minutes on the other side.

5. Quickly put the pan in the hot oven and turn it off. Allow them to rest in the oven without opening it for 10 minutes for a rare steak, or 15 minutes for medium rare steak.

 Romantic Tip:
Plan a romantic trip and you'll discover that half the fun is in the planning.

Christi Silbaugh

Transfer the steaks to a plate, then return the skillet to the stove over medium heat. Add a splash of olive oil and sauté the minced shallots until they start to soften. Add the mushrooms and continue to sauté until they are limp and glossy and there is no liquid in the pan.

7. Add the brandy and swirl it around the bottom of the pan to deglaze. Add the chicken broth and raise the heat to high, boiling until it starts to thicken and there is only about ¼ cup of liquid remaining.

8. Serve the mushrooms and sauce over the steak.

FISH TACOS

I know a lot of people that are afraid to try fish tacos. Don't be afraid. They are so good! They're full of nutrition and pleasing to the taste buds.

Ingredients

1 Tbsp. fresh lime juice

3 Tbsp. olive oil, divided

1 tsp. chili powder

½ tsp. ground cumin

½ tsp. paprika

¼ tsp. salt

½ lb. white fish fillets (halibut, mahi mahi, snapper, tilapia)

for the avocado yogurt sauce:

1 avocados, seeded, peeled and chopped

¼ cup plain greek yogurt

1 Tbsp. fresh lime juice

½ cup cilantro, chopped

¼ tsp. salt

¼ cup water

to assemble:

4 organic corn tortillas

shredded cabbage

cilantro

tomato chopped

Directions

1. In a small bowl, combine the lime juice, 1 tablespoon olive oil, chili powder, cumin, paprika, and salt, stirring until smooth.

2. Pat the fish dry with paper towels. Rub both sides with the lime/pepper marinade. Transfer to a plate and cover tightly with plastic wrap, then transfer to the refrigerator to marinate for 15–20 minutes.

3. While the fish marinates, prepare the avocado yogurt sauce. In the bowl of a food processor, combine all the ingredients until smooth and creamy. Transfer to a serving bowl and cover tightly with plastic wrap. Refrigerate until ready to use.

4. In a large heavy-bottomed skillet set over medium-high heat, sauté the fish in the remaining 2 tablespoons olive oil until opaque and flaky, about 4–5 minutes per side.

 Romantic Tip:

Spend some time outdoors to scope out the perfect private picnic spot. Before you take your love there, find a tree to carve your and your love's initials in, surrounded by a heart. Plan your picnic to be in front of that tree. Your love will live forever, carved into the tree.

Christi Silbaugh

5. Remove from the heat and transfer to a platter. Using a fork, break up each fillet into bite-sized chunks. Cover with foil and set aside while you warm the tortillas.

6. In a heavy-bottomed skillet set over medium heat, warm the tortillas one at a time for 20–30 seconds per side, until soft and flexible. Wrap the finished tortillas with a clean dishcloth to keep them warm between batches.

7. To assemble, place two tortillas on each plate and drizzle with avocado-yogurt sauce. Divide the fish evenly between the tortillas, then serve immediately with bowls of toppings so everyone can top off their tacos as they please.

Main Dishes

HALIBUT GRIBICHE

Gribiche is a mayonnaise-style cold egg sauce in French cuisine, made by emulsifying hard-boiled egg yolks and mustard with canola oil. The sauce is finished with chopped pickles, cucumbers, capers, parsley, tarragon, and chopped hard-boiled egg whites. It's similar to the American tartar sauce. This is a deconstructed gribiche. It's got the same wonderful flavors, but is a whole lot easier and healthier. It is absolutely perfect served with white fish.

Ingredients

for the gribiche:
⅓ cup diced tomato

3 Tbsp. minced shallots

3 Tbsp. minced baby dill pickles

2 Tbsp. capers

¼ cup extra-virgin olive oil

2 Tbsp. sherry vinegar

juice of ½ a lemon

sea salt

freshly ground black pepper

1 tsp. chopped fresh tarragon leaves

1 tsp. fresh parsley

1 green onion, white part only, minced

for the fish:
2 (8-oz.) halibut fillets

1 Tbsp. extra-virgin olive oil

1 Tbsp. garlic powder

½ tsp. paprika

½ tsp. ginger

½ tsp. freshly ground black pepper

½ tsp. dried mustard

½ tsp. oregano

½ tsp. chili powder

1 pinch cayenne pepper

eggs

Directions

1. For the gribiche: Stir the tomato, shallots, pickles, capers, olive oil, vinegar, and lemon juice together in a bowl. Season with salt and pepper. Leave it at room temperature for 2 hours, or put it in the fridge overnight and bring it to room temperature before serving.

2. Preheat the oven to 400 degrees.

3. Prepare a baking dish with non-stick spray or olive oil. In a small bowl, combine the dry seasonings.

4. Drizzle the olive oil over the halibut and rub it down to coat evenly. Mix the dry ingredients together and rub it generously over the fish.

5. For the fish: Bring a skillet to medium heat and add the olive oil to the pan. Fry the fish for 2 minutes on each side, just to sear.

Christi Silbaugh

6. Place the fish on a prepared baking pan. Pour any remaining seasoning over the fillets on the sheet and place the baking pan in the oven.

7. Bake for 10 minutes. While it is baking, poach your eggs. You can fry them if you prefer, but the key here is to just have a runny yolk to place on top of the fish. Serve immediately.

Romantic Tip:

Pamper your love by warming bath towels in the dryer for a few minutes before they need them.

Main Dishes

HERB-CRUSTED SALMON

This is a heart healthy recipe that tastes like it must be bad for you, but it isn't. I served it with a quinoa side, but it would also be great with a brown rice.

Ingredients

¼ cup Parmesan cheese

½ cup fresh parsley

1 Tbsp. olive oil

sea salt

freshly ground black pepper

1 Tbsp. Dijon mustard

1 Tbsp. fresh lemon juice

2 (6–8-oz.) salmon fillets

Directions

1. Preheat the oven to 450 degrees.

2. Line a baking sheet with aluminum foil and set aside.

3. In a large mixing bowl, combine the Parmesan cheese, parsley, and oil, then season the mixture to taste with salt and pepper. Stir until coarse crumbs form.

4. Stir the Dijon and lemon juice together.

5. Place the salmon on prepared sheet and season with salt and pepper.

6. Spread the tops of the fillets with the Dijon lemon mixture.

7. Top the fish with the cheese herb crumb mixture, pressing gently to adhere.

8. Roast until the salmon is opaque throughout, 11–13 minutes.

 Romantic Tip:

Make a "Why I Love You" list of your love's best qualities and jot it down in a simple, handmade card for his or her birthday, anniversary, or just for an everyday surprise.

Main Dishes

LASAGNA BOLOGNESE

This recipe serves 4, because pasta is magnificent leftover. My husband loves to take it to work the next day for lunch and make his office pals jealous with the smell of Italian food.

Ingredients

1 Tbsp. olive oil

½ lb. ground beef

½ lb. ground pork

2 oz. pancetta, diced

½ large onion, chopped

½ carrot, finely chopped

½ celery stalk, finely diced

3 garlic cloves, chopped

sea salt

freshly ground black pepper

½ cup apple cider vinegar

½ cup whole milk

1 (14.5-oz.) can crushed tomatoes

1½ cups chicken broth

½ tsp. sea salt

1½ cups flour

2 large eggs

1 cup finely grated Parmesan cheese

for the béchamel:

2½ Tbsp. unsalted butter

½ cup flour

2 cups whole milk, warmed

Kosher salt

Directions

1. For the bolognese sauce: Pulse the onion, carrot, and celery in a food processor until finely chopped.

2. Heat the olive oil in a large, heavy pot over medium heat. Add the ground beef, ground pork, pancetta, and vegetables. Cook for 25–30 minutes, breaking up ground meat with a spoon, until the moisture is almost completely evaporated and the meat is well browned. Season with salt and pepper.

3. Add the vinegar to the pot and bring to a boil, scraping up the browned bits from bottom of the pot, for about 2 minutes. Add the milk and bring to a boil, reduce the heat, and simmer for 8–10 minutes until the moisture is almost completely evaporated.

4. Add the tomatoes and broth. Bring them to a boil, reduce the heat, and simmer for 2½–3 hours, until the flavors meld and the sauce thickens.

5. Let the sauce cool, then cover and chill it for at least 12 hours, or up to 2 days. (Letting the sauce sit will give it a deeper, richer flavor.)

6. For the pasta dough: Whisk the salt and flour in a large bowl, make a well in the center, and crack the eggs into the well. Mix the eggs with a fork, then slowly mix in the flour until a dough consistent.

7. Turn out the dough onto a lightly floured surface and knead, dusting lightly with flour if it is sticky, for about 5 minutes, until smooth (it will be fairly stiff). Wrap it in

Christi Silbaugh

plastic and let it sit until the dough holds an indentation when pressed, for about one hour. Chill the dough if you are not rolling it out right away. Bring it to room temperature before rolling out.

8. Set your pasta maker to its thickest setting and dust it lightly with flour. Divide the dough into 4 pieces. Working with 1 piece at a time and keeping the remaining dough wrapped in plastic, flatten the dough into a narrow rectangle (no wider than mouth of machine), and pass it through the rollers.

9. Fold the dough as needed to run through one more time. Repeat without folding, adjusting the machine to thinner settings after every pass and dusting with flour if sticky, until the pasta sheet is $\frac{1}{16}$-inch thick (setting 8 on most machines). Place the pasta sheets on a lightly floured surface and cut crosswise into eight 8-inch-long noodles.

10. If you are making the noodles ahead, stack them on a baking sheet with a piece of parchment paper between each layer. Cover them with plastic wrap and chill.

11. For the Béchamel: Heat the butter in a medium saucepan over medium heat until foaming. Add the flour and cook, whisking constantly, for 1 minute.

12. Whisk in the warm milk, ½ of a cupful at a time. Bring the sauce to a boil, reduce the heat, and simmer, whisking often, for 8–10 minutes, until it is the consistency of cream. Add the nutmeg and season with salt. Remove from the heat, transfer to a medium bowl, and press plastic wrap directly onto the surface. Let cool slightly.

13. Cook the noodles. Working in batches, cook the fresh lasagna noodles in a large pot of boiling salted water until just softened, about 10 seconds.

14. Remove carefully with tongs and transfer to a large bowl of ice water to cool. Drain the noodles and stack them on a baking sheet, with paper towels between each layer, making sure the noodles don't touch (they'll stick together).

15. Preheat the oven to 350 degrees. Coat a 9 × 13 baking dish with butter.

16. Assemble the lasagna: Spread ¼ cup of the béchamel in the prepared baking dish. Top with a layer of noodles, spread over a scant ¾ cup Bolognese sauce, then ½ cup béchamel, and top with ¼ cup Parmesan. Repeat this process 7 more times, starting with the noodles and ending with the Parmesan, for a total of 8 layers.

17. Place the baking dish on a rimmed baking sheet and bake the lasagna for 50–60 minutes, until bubbling and beginning to brown on top. Let the lasagna sit for 45 minutes before serving.

LASAGNA CUPS

A cute way to serve lasagna while controlling the serving size. Can be served as the main event, or as a side dish.

Ingredients

4 oz. cream cheese

2 garlic cloves, minced

1 tsp. Italian seasoning

½ tsp. salt

⅛ tsp. pepper

6 lasagna noodles

½ lb. sweet Italian sausage, cooked and drained

1 cup marinara sauce

½ cup Parmesan cheese

1 cup shredded mozzarella cheese

fresh basil garnish for garnish

Directions

1. For the cheese filling: stir together the cream cheese, minced garlic, chopped chives, Italian seasoning, salt, and pepper. Set aside.

2. For the pasta: Bring a large pot of salted water to boil. Cook the pasta sheets for 2 minutes less than package directions and drain. Place the pasta on greased baking sheet until you are ready for assembly.

3. Cook your meat and drain it.

4. For assembly: Preheat the oven to 350 degrees.

5. Cut your noodles in half. Make a cross over each cup in a muffin tin with the noodles. Push the cross down to make a cup shape. I find it easiest to use every other hole in the muffin tins.

6. Spoon about 2 tablespoons of meat into the bottom of each cup. Add 2 tablespoons marinara sauce. Next, add 1 tablespoon of the cream cheese mixture. Top with 2 tablespoons of mozzarella and 1 tablespoon of Parmesan. Finally, top your cups with chopped fresh basil. Repeat this process until you have used all your noodles.

7. Bake for 25–30 minutes or until everything is hot and bubbly.

LEMON DILL SHRIMP AND CORN

This dish is tangy and sweet—the perfect summertime dish. Don't remove the shells! It holds in the marinade and also adds a lot of flavor. Wait to remove them until you eat them.

Ingredients

1 lb. large shrimp or prawns

1 bay leaf

½ Tbsp. lightly crushed black peppercorns

1 lemon, quartered

2 ears sweet corn kernels, cut from the cob

2 sprigs fresh majoram

1 serrano chile pepper

½ cup sliced green onions

for the vinaigrette:

¼ cup fresh lemon juice

2 Tbsp. minced dill

2 Tbsp. white vinegar

1 tsp. sugar

¼ cup olive oil

sea salt

freshly ground black pepper

Directions

1. First, make the vinaigrette. Add all the ingredients to a bowl or measuring cup and stir until combined.

2. Next, butterfly the shrimp using a small serrated knife. Make a shallow cut, just enough to remove the vein from the shrimp. Keep the shells on and rinse with cold water.

3. In a large saucepan, place the shrimp in just enough water to cover them. Add the bay leaf, peppercorns, and the lemon, squeezed.

4. Bring to a boil over moderately high heat. The second it starts boiling, add the corn, marjoram, and chile and stir once, stir again, and remove from the heat. Drain immediately, discarding the hot water and bay leaf, and pour the remaining contents into a serving bowl. Fold in the green onions. Pour the vinaigrette over the corn and shrimp.

5. Let stand for 10–12 minutes at room temperature, tossing occasionally. Remove the marjoram sprigs, season, and serve.

Romantic Tip:

Try doing a selfless act for your partner. Do they hate taking the trash out? Emptying the dishwasher? Do a task for them that they dislike, just because you love them. Don't point it out. Do it just because, without expecting anything in return.

Christi Silbaugh

NEGIMAKI

Negimaki is a Japanese food consisting of broiled strips of beef—marinated in sauce and rolled with green onions. If your mate loves steak, serve them this tasty Asian twist.

Ingredients

⅛ cup tamari

⅛ cup mirin

¾ Tbsp. brown rice miso

½ Tbsp. agave nectar

¼ tsp. sesame oil

¾ lb. ¼-in. thick slices of tenderloin steak, pounded ⅛-in. thick

¼ lb. kale, stems discarded

4 green onions

vegetable oil for brushing

sesame seeds for garnish (optional)

Romantic Tip:

Let loose, act silly, be a little crazy. How can being silly make for a romantic interlude? By being silly, you make yourself vulnerable, and show off how comfortable you are with being you. Dance, sing, make people stare. The point here is that you are having fun, and your significant other will want to share in the fun with you.

Directions

1. In a small bowl, whisk together the tamari, mirin, miso, agave, and sesame oil. Spread 1 teaspoon of the mixture on each side of the beef slices. Refrigerate for 1 hour. Reserve the remaining marinade.

2. In a saucepan of salted boiling water, cook the kale until bright green, about 2 minutes. Drain and lightly squeeze out the excess water.

3. Lay out a slice of beef with the long side facing you. Place 1 green onion slice across the lower edge. Top with ¼ of the kale; some of the kale should extend beyond the short sides of the meat. Roll the meat up over the filling very tightly. Secure the roll with 2 toothpicks. Repeat with the remaining meat, green onions, and kale.

4. Light a grill or preheat a grill pan. Brush the negimaki rolls with oil. Oil the grill grate. Grill the rolls for 2 minutes over high heat until charred. Brush the rolls with some marinade and grill for a few seconds more, until glazed.

5. Transfer the rolls to a work surface. Discard the toothpicks. Cut the negimaki into 1-inch lengths. Transfer to a platter, cut the sides up, and drizzle with the remaining marinade. Sprinkle with sesame seeds and serve.

ORANGE CHICKEN

Forget your fast food orange chicken. Try this made-from-scratch recipe and you'll never go out for Asian food again.

Ingredients

1 lb. boneless, skinless chicken thighs

¼ cup cornstarch

¾ tsp. sea salt

⅛ tsp. white pepper

1 egg

1 Tbsp. canola oil (or other low saturated fat oil) for frying

for the sauce:

¾ Tbsp. soy sauce

¾ Tbsp. rice vinegar

3 Tbsp. agave nectar

1 Tbsp. canola oil

½ Tbsp. minced garlic

½ Tbsp. minced fresh ginger

⅛ cup chopped green onion

¼ tsp. red pepper flakes

½ Tbsp. mirin

¼ tsp. sesame oil

⅛ cup water

1 Tbsp. cornstarch

Romantic Tip:

Put a note on the remote. "Leave the TV off and come turn me on." It will be the start of a special evening.

Directions

1. Cut the chicken thighs into bite-sized pieces.

2. Mix the cornstarch, salt, and pepper. Beat the egg in a small bowl with the oil. Mix into the cornstarch mixture. Add the cornstarch/egg mixture to the chicken in the bowl and coat well.

3. Heat enough oil to fry in a large, deep skillet or wok. Heat the oil to 375 degrees. Fry the chicken in batches so there is plenty of room left around the chicken.

4. Fry the chicken on each side for 5–7 minutes or until crisp and beginning to brown. Drain with a slotted spoon and place on a paper towel-lined plate. Repeat until all the chicken is cooked.

5. Mix the soy sauce, rice vinegar, and agave in a small bowl. Set aside.

6. In an extra large skillet or wok, add another tablespoon of oil. Add the minced garlic and ginger and stir fry until very aromatic—maybe 15 seconds. Add the green onion and the pepper flakes and stir fry for 10 seconds.

7. Stir the soy sauce mixture in the bowl and add it to the wok. Bring the sauce to a boil. Add the mirin and the sesame oil. Mix the ¼ cup water and cornstarch and add to the boiling sauce, stirring constantly until sauce is thickened and bubbling. Add the cooked chicken, coating it well with the sauce.

8. Serve immediately. It tastes great over rice.

Christi Silbaugh

OVERNIGHT STEEL-CUT OATS

I like to send my man off to work with a full belly. My husband loves steel-cut oats for breakfast. The problem is, they usually take ages to cook. Not anymore! A few minutes in the evening turns into a healthy, stick-to-your-ribs breakfast for my man.

Ingredients

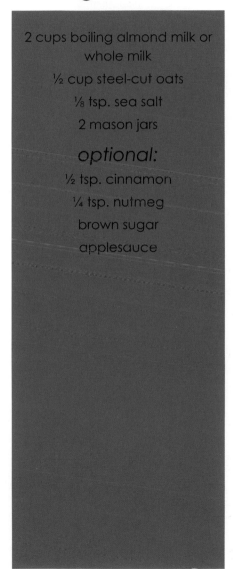

2 cups boiling almond milk or whole milk

½ cup steel-cut oats

⅛ tsp. sea salt

2 mason jars

optional:

½ tsp. cinnamon

¼ tsp. nutmeg

brown sugar

applesauce

Directions

1. Add 1 cup of the boiling almond milk, ¼ cup of the steel-cut oats, and a pinch of salt to each mason jar.

2. Cover the mason jars with their lids and shake. Let them stand overnight. If you can, give them a shake or two when you think about it.

3. The next morning, shake the jars, remove the lids, and add optional add-ins: stevia, applesauce, or fruit. Heat in the microwave for 5 minutes, or reheat over the stove for 5 minutes.

4. Top with brown sugar, stevia, fruit, or whatever you'd like!

 Romantic Tip:

Spark is important to maintain. Without a spark, the fire slowly dies! The important thing to remember is your partner needs and wants you to excite him as much as you want them to excite you. I don't care what your body type is, your husband wants to see it. They would not be with you if they didn't. I am just as self conscious as the next person, but coming out in a sexy outfit full of confidence will drive your partner crazy.

Main Dishes

PARMESAN DILL SEA BASS

You can put this dish together in 20 minutes and it's so simple and so tasty. Try it as an alternative to fish and chips—it's just as tasty, with half the calories. The recipe will work well with any flaky white fish; just adjust the baking time according to the thickness of the fish.

Ingredients

¼ cup milk
2 (6-8-oz.) sea bass fillets
½ cup Parmesan cheese
2 Tbsp. fresh dill, chopped
1 Tbsp. canola oil
½ lemon, cut into wedges
1 Tbsp. butter, melted

Directions

1. Preheat the oven to 375 degrees and spray a large baking dish with cooking spray.

2. Pour the milk into a ziploc bag, add the sea bass, and shake the bag to coat the fish.

3. On a large plate, add the Parmesan cheese and the dill and mix it all together.

4. Take each piece of the sea bass and dredge it in the Parmesan mixture. Turn the fish to evenly coat each side, pressing firmly.

5. Put a skillet with the canola oil over medium heat. Press the sea bass down firmly in the skillet to sear, for about 2 minutes on each side.

6. Place each sea bass fillet into the baking dish. Take a wedge of the lemon and squeeze the juice over the top of each fillet—one wedge per fillet. Place ½ tablespoon of the butter on top of each fillet. Place the baking dish in the oven and bake for 18 minutes.

Romantic Tip:

Pick out a book and read it aloud together. This will result in quality time together, and the expansion of your individual and collective knowledge bases.

Christi Silbaugh

PORK TAMALES

If you are like me, this recipe looks daunting. It isn't. You just need to plan out the steps. Several of them can be done the day before—I chose to cook the pork and make the cream the day before. Don't be intimidated by these tamales!

Ingredients

for the cilantro lime crema:

2 Tbsp. chopped fresh cilantro

1 Tbsp. chicken stock

½ Tbsp. lime juice

⅛ tsp. salt

4 oz. sour cream

1 garlic clove, minced

for the pork:

½ Tbsp. olive oil

1½ lb. pork shoulder

¼ tsp. salt

½ cup chopped onion

4 garlic cloves, chopped

½ tsp. cumin

3 chipotle chiles

½ cup chicken stock

½ tsp. grated orange rind

½ tsp. cocoa powder

⅛ tsp. ground coffee

corn husks

for the masa filling:

1¼ cups chicken stock

1 ancho chile, seeded and finely chopped

½ cup corn kernels

2 cups instant masa harina

¾ tsp. salt

¾ tsp. baking soda

¼ cup crisco

Directions

1. To prepare the crema, stir all the ingredients together and chill for at least one hour, overnight if possible.

2. To prepare the pork, add all the pork ingredients to a crock-pot and cook on low for 7 hours, or on high for 4 hours.

3. Shred the pork and return it to the crock-pot.

4. Immerse the corn husks in water. Soak them for 30 minutes and drain.

5. Preheat your oven to 450 degrees.

6. To prepare the masa filling, combine the stock and the chile in a microwave-safe bowl. Microwave on high for 2 minutes or until the chiles are tender. Cool slightly.

Romantic Tip:

Write a love letter to your partner. Open yourself up and share your deepest thoughts about your love on paper. It's sure to make them feel extra special.

Christi Silbaugh

7. Combine the hot stock, chiles, and corn in a blender and process until smooth. Combine the masa harina, salt, and baking soda, stirring well with a whisk. Cut in the crisco with a pastry blender or two knives, until the mixture resembles coarse meal.

8. Add the ancho mixture to the masa mixture and stir until a soft dough forms.

9. Turn the dough out onto a lightly floured surface, then knead it until it is smooth and pliable.

10. To assemble the tamales: Working with one husk at a time (or overlap 2 small husks), place about 3 tablespoons of the masa mixture in the center of the husk, about 1 inch from the top of husk. Press the dough into a 4 × 3-inch rectangle.

11. Spoon about 1 heaping tablespoon of the pork mixture into the middle of the dough.

12. Using the corn husk as your guide, fold the husk over the tamale, being sure to cover the filling with the dough. Use the husk to seal the masa around the filling. Tear 3 or 4 corn husks lengthwise into strips and use them to tie the ends of the tamale.

13. Place the tamale seam side down on the rack of a broiler pan lined with a damp towel.

14. Repeat the procedure with the remaining husks, masa mixture, and pork mixture. Cover the tamales with a damp towel. Pour 2 cups of hot water into the bottom of a broiler pan, setting the rack on top.

15. Steam the tamales at 450 degrees for 25 minutes. Remove, re-wet the top towel, and add 1 cup of water to the pan. Turn the tamales over and top with the cloth. Bake for 20 minutes or until set. Let the tamales stand for 10 minutes. Serve the tamales with the crema.

SCALLOPS WITH BEURRE BLANC OVER ORZO

This gourmet meal is so easy to make, yet it looks and tastes like it came from a high-end restaurant.

Ingredients

for the beurre blanc:
½ cup white wine vinegar

1 Tbsp. agave nectar

1 shallot, minced

½ Tbsp. heavy whipping cream

¾ cup cold butter, cubed

freshly ground black pepper

for the orzo:
¼ lb. dried orzo

½ Tbsp. olive oil

¼ lemon, zest and juice

1 Tbsp. chopped chives

for the scallops:
10 fresh large scallops

sea salt

freshly ground black pepper

1 Tbsp. canola or vegetable oil

Directions

1. For the beurre blanc: Bring the wine vinegar, agave, and shallot to a boil in a medium stainless steel saucepan. Cook the mixture until it has reduced to a very thick glaze for 8–12 minutes, depending on the size of the pan.

2. Strain the sauce through a fine mesh sieve, discarding the solids, and return the liquid to the saucepan.

3. Remove the pan from the heat and stir in the cream.

4. Vigorously whisk in the butter, cube by cube, not adding another piece until the last is almost fully melted. The sauce should be thick, creamy, and glossy.

5. Season with pepper to taste. Hold on the lowest heat, stirring occasionally, until ready to serve.

6. While the beurre blanc is reducing, cook the orzo according to the package directions. Drain well. Toss with the olive oil, lemon juice, lemon zest, and chives. Season with salt and pepper.

Romantic Tip:

Fall in love with your partner's hobby for a day. Is there something they love to do that you use your "hall pass" for every time they mention it? This time, just go with it! Take up their hobby for a day and show interest in something they love. Who knows, maybe you'll like it too!

Christi Silbaugh

7. For the scallops: Heat a cast iron skillet over medium-high heat.

8. While the pan is heating, pat the scallops and dust them with sea salt and pepper. Add the oil to the pan. Once it is shimmery and hot, arrange the scallops, salted side down, around the outside of the pan. Once they are in the pan, dust the tops with salt and pepper.

9. Allow the scallops to sear, undisturbed, for a minute or so. When you start to see a golden brown crust beginning to rise up the side of a scallop, it is ready to flip. Once the scallops are flipped, continue cooking for about another minute or so, until they are firm but still a tad uncooked in the center (they will finish cooking with the residual heat). Transfer the scallops to a plate, lined with a paper towel to soak up any cooking juices.

10. Assemble the dish: Begin with orzo, then the scallops, topped with the beurre blanc.

SHEPHERD'S PIE

This is the perfect dish for a rainy night. Meat and potatoes, a comfy blanket, and just the two of you. Does it get any better than that?

Ingredients

½ Tbsp. olive oil

½ onion, finely chopped

½ carrot, finely chopped

1 celery stalk, diced

½ lb. ground beef

1 cup beef stock

½ Tbsp. dried oregano

1 sprig fresh thyme

½ Tbsp. parsley

½ Tbsp. Worcestershire sauce

½ Tbsp. soy sauce

1 Tbsp. tomato paste

sea salt

freshly ground black pepper

3 large russet potatoes, peeled and chopped

2 Tbsp. Butter

¼ cup milk

Romantic Tip:

Communicate. Take time to talk about your goals, your dreams, your plans for the future, your current lives, things you're happy about, things you love about the other person, things you'd like to work on, and things you're grateful for.

Directions

1. Preheat oven to 350 degrees.

2. In a large saucepan, heat the olive oil and add the onion, carrot, and celery. Cook until the onion becomes transparent.

3. Add the ground beef and cook until browned.

4. Add the stock, oregano, parsley, thyme, Worcestershire sauce, soy sauce, tomato paste, salt, and pepper and mix well. Transfer the mixture to a mini springform pan, small ovenproof skillet, mini pie pan, or a small baking dish. Cover with foil and bake in the oven for 1 hour.

5. While the mixture is in the oven, cook the potato in a saucepan of salted boiling water until tender. Drain well and return to the pot, mashing until smooth. Add the butter and milk and stir well until they are completely incorporated. Taste and season with salt and pepper.

6. Remove the dish from oven and increase the temperature to 400 degrees. Discard the foil and top the mixture with the mashed potatoes.

7. Return the pie to the oven, uncovered, and bake for an additional 20 minutes or until the mashed potatoes are golden.

SPICY RED SNAPPER OVER LEMON RICE

The flavors in this dish scream everything my husband and I love. It was also a plus that I used fresh-caught snapper. My husband said it was one of the best meals I have ever made, and I loved it too. Remember, it is spicy!

Ingredients

2 (8-oz.) red snapper fillets

for the marinade:

7 dried red chile's de-seeded and soaked

4 whole black peppercorns

2 tsp. cumin seeds

3 Tbsp. chopped garlic

½ tsp. sugar or agave nectar

1 Tbsp. coriander

½ tsp. tumeric

sea salt

1 Tbsp. canola or other high-temperature oil

for the lemon rice:

1 cup basmati rice

1 Tbsp. canola oil (or other low saturated fat oil)

1 tsp. mustard seeds

2 bay leaves

1 large red onion, minced

1 jalapeño pepper, minced

sea salt to taste

½ tsp. curry powder

½ tsp. turmeric

juice of 1 lemon

handful of chopped cilantro

Directions

1. For the fish marinade: Add all the ingredients in a food processor and blend them until they form a smooth paste. Massage it onto to the fish and let it sit for about an hour.

2. For the lemon rice: Cook your rice according to the directions on the package (usually this is 1 cup of rice to 2 cups water, and 1 teaspoon of salt).

3. Heat the oil in a frying pan over medium-high heat. Add the mustard seeds. When they begin to splutter, add the bay leaves, onions, and jalapeño.

4. Fry for about 2 minutes and add the rice.

5. Sprinkle in the salt, curry, and turmeric and mix well. Fry for about 5 minutes more on medium flame. Turn off the heat, add the lemon juice and cilantro, and mix well.

6. Add 1 tablespoon canola oil to a hot skillet. Add your marinated snapper. Cook for about 2 minutes on each side on high heat, or until cooked through.

7. Serve on a bed of hot lemon rice.

 Romantic Tip:

Surprise your love with an early-morning date. Watch the sky light up, go to a favorite breakfast spot, and start the day with a full plate of companionship.

Christi Silbaugh

SRIRACHA SALMON

I love to cook fish because it can be put together quickly, but it looks and tastes like it came from a 5 star restaurant. Take a bow when you serve your love this delectable dish.

Ingredients

2 (6-8-oz.) fresh salmon fillets

½ cup tamari sauce

2 green onions, chopped

for the sriracha cream sauce:

⅛ cup sriracha

½ cup plain greek yogurt

½ Tbsp. vinegar

¼ tsp. sea salt

¼ tsp. pepper

1½ Tbsp. condensed milk

Directions

1. In a baking dish, place the salmon fillets and add the tamari sauce.

2. Let the marinade reach up the sides of fillets. Marinate the fish in the refrigerator for at least 30 minutes, up to overnight.

3. Preheat the oven to 400 degrees.

4. In a medium bowl, combine the sriracha, Greek yogurt, vinegar, salt, and pepper. Whisk well. Add the condensed milk and whisk until fully incorporated. Add more condensed milk for a milder taste and more sriracha for a spicier taste.

5. Cover the baking dish with the fillets with a sheet of foil and bake at 400 degrees for 20–25 minutes.

6. After baking, place the fish in a serving dish. Drizzle with the sriracha cream sauce and garnish with thinly sliced green onions.

Romantic Tip:
Giving back to the community and helping the less fortunate is something we should all be doing. It is uplifting and makes us realize how much we all need to lend a hand. Talk to your love about volunteering somewhere together. Spend time looking at a cause that touches you, then show up and work hard together. You'll be surprised how much it brings you together.

Main Dishes

STICKY GARLIC CHICKEN

For me there is nothing better than good old comfort food. In my house we love chicken and rice. Add garlic and a good sauce, and it is a sure hit.

Ingredients

1 Tbsp. canola oil

4 garlic cloves, chopped

½ tsp. freshly minced ginger root

1 lb. boneless and skinless chicken thighs

½ cup water

2 Tbsp. soy sauce

2 Tbsp. brown sugar

¼ tsp. Chinese five-spice powder

1 tsp. cornstarch

1 Tbsp. water

Directions

1. Add the canola oil to a wok, then sauté the garlic and ginger for 1 minute.

2. Chop up your chicken and add it to the wok, cooking over high heat for 2 minutes and stirring constantly.

3. Pour in the water, soy sauce, brown sugar, and five-spice powder. Bring it to a boil, then simmer uncovered on medium-high heat until the chicken is cooked through.

4. Strain the chicken, letting the liquid drain into another saucepan or skillet. Remove the chicken and keep it warm while returning the liquid back to the stove top.

5. Whisk the cornstarch and water together to make a paste, then add it to the liquid in the pan. Cook over medium-high heat, stirring occasionally. Mix for 20 minutes, or until the liquid had reduced to a thick syrup texture.

6. Reduce liquid into a thick sauce, pour it over the chicken, and stir.

7. Serve over white rice, top with extra sauce, and serve.

Romantic Tip:

I think it is important to stay connected to your love during the day. Give them a call and let them know you are thinking of them.

Main Dishes

THAI COCONUT LEMON LIME SHRIMP

I would highly recommend getting fresh shrimp if you can. It makes a huge difference. I also like to leave the tails on, because I feel it adds more flavor to the broth.

Ingredients

½ lb. large shrimp or prawns

2 Tbsp. sweet chili sauce

½ lemon, juiced

½ lime, juiced

½ tsp. sriracha

½ tsp. fish sauce

2 garlic cloves, chopped

½ tsp. brown sugar

⅛ cup coconut milk

⅛ cup Thai basil, chopped

Directions

1. Wash, peel, and devein your shrimp, leaving the tails on if possible.

2. Mix together all the remaining ingredients except the coconut milk and Thai basil.

3. Marinate the shrimp in the sauce for 10 minutes.

4. Heat a pan over medium heat. Add the shrimp, the marinade, the coconut milk, and the chopped Thai basil, and simmer for 2–3 minutes until the shrimp are cooked.

5. Serve hot.

Romantic Tip:

When is the last time you stopped and reflected on the things you love about your partner? Putting all negative traits behind, write down what you absolutely love. For example, I love how hard working my husband is. He is not lazy and he does his best each day to provide for us.

I think it is so important to focus on the positive, and having it written down as a reminder can be a very uplifting thing for both of you. Try it!

Christi Silbaugh

THAI RED CURRY CHICKEN

Bringing together the coconut, curry, and peppers makes these Thai flavors dance on your taste buds. Get ready for a flavor explosion in your mouth!

Ingredients

½ Tbsp. canola oil (or other low saturated fat oil)

½ sweet onion, thinly sliced

1 garlic clove, minced

1 Tbsp. red curry paste

3 cups chicken broth

7½ oz. coconut milk

½ Tbsp. fish sauce

7 oz. rice noodles

½ red bell pepper, thinly sliced

1 jalapeño pepper, thinly sliced, divided

½ lb. boneless beef round steak, cut into thin strips diagonally

½ cup fresh cilantro, chopped

lime wedges

Romantic Tip:
Life comes at you fast. Take a few moments out of your day today to nurture your relationship.

Directions

1. Put a large pot (that has a lid for later use) on the stove with the canola oil on medium-high heat. Add the onion slices and cook them until they are soft and lightly browned.

2. Add the garlic and curry paste to the pot and stir them together. After a few minutes add the chicken broth, coconut milk, and fish sauce. Cover with the lid and bring everything to a boil.

3. Add water to another pot and bring it to a boil. Remove from the heat and add the rice noodles. Let it sit for 7 minutes.

4. While the noodles are cooking, add the bell pepper and ½ of the jalapeño pepper to the first pot and lower it to a simmer.

5. Add the chicken and let the soup simmer, uncovered, for 5 minutes. It only takes a little bit of time because the chicken is extremely thinly cut. If you do not cut your chicken thin, this may take longer.

6. Strain the noodles and add them in individual servings to bowls.

7. Pour the chicken and broth mixture over the noodles.

8. Serve with the remaining jalapeño slices, freshly chopped cilantro, and lime wedges.

Main Dishes

WHITE ENCHILADAS

Yummy gooey enchiladas that will be gobbled up fast! They are easy to make too!

Ingredients

6 corn tortillas

1 cup shredded cooked chicken

1 cup Monterey Jack cheese

2 Tbsp. butter

1 Tbsp. flour

1 cup chicken broth

½ cup sour cream or plain Greek yogurt

2 oz. diced green chili peppers

Directions

1. Preheat the oven to 350 degrees and grease a small baking pan.

2. Soften your corn tortillas. I do this in a tortilla warmer, but you can wrap them in a damp paper towel and microwave them for 30 seconds, or you can wrap them in foil and place them in the oven until they are warm. However you like to do it is fine.

3. Mix together the chicken and ½ cup cheese.

4. Roll up the chicken and the cheese mixture in the tortillas and place them in the baking pan.

5. In a saucepan, melt the butter, stir in the flour, and cook for 1 minute. Add the broth and whisk until smooth. Heat over medium heat until thick and bubbly.

6. Stir in the sour cream and chilies. Do not bring to boil; you don't want curdled sour cream.

7. Pour over the enchiladas and top with the remaining cheese.

8. Bake for 20 min and then under high broil for 3–5 minutes to brown the cheese. Serve!

 Romantic Tip:

Slow dance to romantic music with your love.

Christi Silbaugh

SIDE DISHES

Asian Beans

Asian Coleslaw

Breadsticks

Buttermilk Biscuits

Chicken Fried Quinoa

Cranberry Sauce

Creamy Garlic Pasta

Garlic Fried Rice

Garlic Mashed Potato
   Cupcakes

Garlic Parmesan Fries

Garlic Parmesan Knots

Grilled Garlic and
   Herb Shrimp

Hollandaise Sauce

Irish Soda Bread

Kung Pao Cauliflower

Latkes

Loaded Mashed Potato Cakes

Oven-Roasted Garlic
   Mushrooms

Parmesan Roasted Cauliflower

Potato Gratin

ASIAN BEANS

I personally believe that this is the best way to serve green beans. If you have ever ordered them at an Asian restaurant, you know what I am talking about!

Ingredients

2 tsp. canola oil

6 garlic cloves, thinly sliced

1 lb. green beans, washed

1 Tbsp. sesame oil

2 Tbsp. soy sauce

⅛ tsp. white pepper

1 tsp. ginger

3 dried red chili peppers

1 Tbsp. toasted sesame seeds

sea salt

freshly ground black pepper

Directions

1. Heat a large pan or wok over medium heat. Pour in the canola oil and add the sliced garlic. Cook for 1–2 minutes, stirring constantly to prevent burning.

2. Toss in the green beans and sesame oil. Stir the beans to coat with the oil. Add the soy sauce, white pepper, ginger, and chili peppers.

3. Cook for about 8–10 minutes, until the beans are bright green. Stir in the toasted sesame seeds and salt and pepper to taste. Transfer to a serving platter and serve.

 Romantic Tip:

Pack your travel bags and get away from it all during the weekend with a surprise vacation for your love.

ASIAN COLESLAW

This spicy asian slaw is sure to knock your socks off. My husband loves heat, so I leave the seeds in the serrano when I cut it. If you only like mild heat, you can remove the seeds.

Ingredients

2 Tbsp. canola oil

2 Tbsp. fish sauce

2 Tbsp. fresh lime juice

2 Tbsp. rice vinegar

½ Tbsp. sugar

½ Tbsp. chopped garlic

1 serrano pepper, chopped

1 Tbsp. chopped fresh mint

½ head of cabbage

1 cup grated carrots

Directions

1. Mix the first 7 ingredients (through the peppers) together and whisk well.

2. Toss together the carrots, mint, and cabbage.

3. Pour the wet ingredients over the vegetable mixture and toss.

4. Refrigerate until ready to use. I stir mine every 30 minutes or so to make sure the flavors are well distributed. Strain the coleslaw prior to serving.

Romantic Tip:

Do you play board games? Call me silly and old fashioned if you must, but my husband and I do. Want to know the funny thing? It helps our love life. We find we talk more, laugh more, and flirt more when we play games. At the end of the day a lot of people just switch on the television. We try to limit our TV intake and spend our time living our lives rather than watching other people live theirs. It brings us close together. With the vast selection of games out there for two people to play, you will find something you both enjoy.

Christi Silbaugh

BREADSTICKS

You will be surprised to learn these are very easy to make. You don't need to be a star baker or have special equipment. They are ready in a little over an hour. So go on! Get baking!

Ingredients

1 tsp. sugar

1 tsp. active dry yeast

¼ cup warm water (115-120°F)

¾ cup flour

1 pinch sea salt

1 tsp. butter, melted

for the topping:

2 Tbsp. butter

½ tsp. garlic powder

1 pinch salt

Romantic Tip:
No matter how busy you get, remember to say "I love you" and "I need you" often.

Directions

1. In a bowl, dissolve the sugar and yeast in warm water and allow it to sit for 10 minutes, covered. The mixture should be frothy.

2. In separate large mixing bowl, combine the flour and salt. Add the yeast mixture, then the melted butter. Mix with paddle attachment of a stand mixer, or a wooden spoon, until fully combined. Knead the dough for a few minutes, just until the dough is smooth.

3. Grease a cookie sheet. Pull off pieces of the dough and roll them out into strips. Cover the dough and let it sit in a warm place for 45 minutes to an hour. I use my heating pad for a perfect warm temperature.

4. Preheat your oven to 400 degrees. Once it is finished preheating, pop in the bread sticks.

5. In microwave or on stovetop, melt the butter for the topping and mix together your topping ingredients.

6. After the breadsticks have cooked for 6–7 minutes, brush them with ½ of the butter mixture. Then continue to bake for 5–8 more minutes.

7. Immediately upon removal from the oven, brush the other half of the butter on the sticks. Allow to cool for a few minutes before eating.

BUTTERMILK BISCUITS

These biscuits are so easy to throw together and they are so flaky and tasty!

Ingredients

1½ cups flour

¾ Tbsp. baking powder

¼ tsp. salt

5 Tbsp. unsalted butter, cold, cut into small pieces

½ cup buttermilk

2 Tbsp. butter, melted

Directions

1. Preheat the oven to 450 degrees.

2. In a large bowl, whisk together the flour, baking powder, and salt. Add the butter and cut it in with a pastry blender, a paddle attachment, or your fingers until the mixture resembles coarse crumbs and the largest pieces are pea-sized.

3. Add the buttermilk all at once and mix it in with a rubber spatula or wooden spoon until just combined.

4. Knead the dough in the bowl 2 or 3 times, folding the dough over itself into a rough ball, then transfer it to a lightly floured surface. Roll or pat it out to ½-inch thick.

5. Cut into rounds with a biscuit or cookie cutter dipped in flour.

6. Melt the butter in a cast iron skillet. Place the rounds in the buttered cast iron skillet.

7. Bake in your preheated oven for 10–12 minutes or until the biscuits are golden brown on top and a deeper golden brown on the bottom.

 Romantic Tip:
The next time you're walking together, grab your love's hand or walk arm-in-arm.

Christi Silbaugh

CHICKEN FRIED QUINOA

Since quinoa is full of protein and has less calories and carbs than rice, this dish is much healthier than traditional fried rice. This packed-with-protein side dish could easily be the main dish in my mind.

Ingredients

2 cups cooked quinoa

4 cups vegetable broth or water

½ tsp. canola oil (or other low saturated fat oil), divided

½ Tbsp. butter

½ Tbsp. minced garlic

sea salt to taste

freshly ground black pepper to taste

¼ cup chopped onion

1 Tbsp. chopped green onions, plus extra for garnish

¼ cup finely chopped carrots

⅛ cup soy sauce

1 egg

½ tsp. sea salt

1 dash black pepper

Romantic Tip:
Take time out to enjoy each other. A day off from duties can be very rewarding.

Directions

1. Cook your quinoa according to the package directions. I like to cook mine in vegetable broth instead of water for added flavor. I use 2 parts broth to one part quinoa, simmering until all the broth is absorbed. Set aside.

2. Heat a non-stick skillet over medium heat. Add ½ tsp. oil, butter, garlic, and sprinkle with salt and pepper.

3. Add the remaining oil to the pan and raise the heat to medium-high. Sauté the onion, green onion, and carrots for 2-3 minutes, until tender. Move to the side of the pan.

4. Add the beaten eggs to the skillet and scramble until firm.

5. Mix together the quinoa, scrambled eggs, salt, pepper, and veggies, stirring well.

6. Add the soy sauce to the mixture. Let it cook for a few minutes, then flip it over. Cook it for another few minutes until it becomes a little crispy.

7. Stir the mixture together. Top with green onions for a garnish and serve!

CRANBERRY SAUCE

Don't just serve cranberry sauce on Thanksgiving. It is also great in grilled cheese sandwiches, with baked Brie, as a mixer in drinks, and much more.

Ingredients

12 oz. fresh cranberries
¼ cup fresh blueberries
¼ cup fresh raspberries
1 cup water
¾ cup agave nectar
½ orange, zest only

Directions

1. Pick over your cranberries, removing any wilted or damaged ones.

2. Rinse them to clean them off, along with the rest of the berries, and place them all in a saucepan with the water and agave nectar.

3. Bring everything to a simmer. Then lightly mash it with a potato masher. Leave the texture; don't completely mash the berries.

4. Remove the mixture from the heat and let it cool to room temperature.

5. Add your orange zest, mix the sauce, and place it in the refrigerator, allowing the sauce to thicken.

6. If kept in an airtight container, it will keep in the fridge for up to 2 weeks.

Romantic Tip:

Spend an entire day anticipating your partners wants. What are their favorite foods? What would they love to see when they come home? If they wrote down their perfect day for you, what would be on that list? Think about that and then do as many things on that list as possible.

Christi Silbaugh

CREAMY GARLIC PASTA

This recipe is like a noodle-roni, but with wholesome ingredients, not powders and fillers.

Ingredients

2 tsp. extra virgin olive oil

2 Tbsp. butter

4 garlic cloves, minced

¼ tsp. sea salt

3 cups chicken stock or broth

8 oz. dried linguine noodles

8 oz. Parmesan cheese

½ cup heavy whipping cream

2 Tbsp. chopped fresh parsley

Directions

1. In a large stock pot, heat the olive oil and butter over medium heat.

2. When the butter has melted, add the garlic and cook until fragrant, about 1 minute.

3. Add the salt and chicken stock to the pan. Raise the heat to high and bring the stock to a boil.

4. Break the linguine in half and add it to the chicken stock. Cook according to the package directions.

5. Reduce the heat to medium and add the cheese to the pasta, stirring to combine.

6. When cheese has melted, remove the pasta from the heat and stir in the cream and parsley.

 Romantic Tip:

There is no such thing of a couple that doesn't fight. But is the fight worth the relationship? Take time to think about that the next time you are so mad that steam is coming out of your ears. If it is worth ending the relationship over, then by all means, hold your ground. But if it is a regular fight, how about swallowing your pride, asking for forgiveness, and then move on to a wonderful evening together? Be the first to say "I'm sorry" and kiss and make up.

Sides

GARLIC FRIED RICE

This rice is very buttery and full of garlic flavor. The crunchy garlic on top turns this dish into a must-have!

Ingredients

2 Tbsp. butter

6 garlic cloves, chopped

3 eggs, lightly beaten

1½ cups cooked basmati rice

sea salt to taste

freshly ground black pepper to taste

green onions, chopped for garnish

Directions

1. Melt 1 tablespoon of the butter in a large pan or wok. Add in 3 cloves of the chopped garlic and stir until very fragrant and lightly golden.

2. While waiting for the butter and garlic, add the beaten egg to the rice and mix well.

3. Add this rice mixture to the pan or wok. Toss together, then add salt and pepper. Toss again.

4. In another small saucepan, melt the remaining tablespoon of butter and the rest of the chopped garlic. Sauté until the garlic is browned nicely.

5. Assemble the rice and garnish it with some chopped green onions and browned garlic.

Romantic Tip:

When is the last time you picked up a book of poetry? Maybe in this day and age you need to Google poetry, or download poetry on your Kindle, Nook, iPad, or whatever tickles your fancy. Read a romantic poem or two with your love. It makes you think, and automatically creates a romantic mood.

Christi Silbaugh

GARLIC MASHED POTATO CUPCAKES

One of my favorite things to eat is good, buttery garlic mashed potatoes. Since they are full of fat and calories, a need to control portion size is bigger than ever. Cupcake liners = problem solved! They have a great presentation and are perfectly portioned.

Ingredients

½ lb. russet potatoes, peeled and diced

¼ cup butter

8 oz. cream cheese

2 Tbsp. half-and-half

½ tsp. sea salt

⅛ tsp. freshly ground black pepper

6 garlic cloves, minced

minced flat leaf parsley for garnish

Directions

1. Bring a pot of water to a simmer and add the potatoes. Bring it to a boil and cook for 30 minutes.

2. Drain the potatoes in a large colander. When the potatoes have finished draining, place them back into the dry pot and put the pot on the stove. Mash the potatoes over low heat, allowing all the steam to escape before adding in the other ingredients.

3. Turn off the stove and add the butter, garlic, cream cheese, and half-and-half. Then whip or mash them. I find whipping makes them light and fluffy, but make sure you don't over-whip.

4. Add the salt and black pepper.

5. Mix well and place in 4 baking cups. I like to pipe my potatoes in so they look like frosting.

6. Sprinkle the potatoes with parsley and serve.

7. You can make these ahead of time and reheat them in a 350 degree oven until warm.

 Romantic Tip:
Sometimes we all just need some time out to have a good laugh. Get out and go to a funny movie, live play, or comedy club once in a while and let your cares drift away for a few hours.

Sides

GARLIC PARMESAN FRIES

These are my ultimate comfort food. If fries are your thing, but you are trying to avoid the high calorie version, these baked fries are just as good, if not better!

Ingredients

3 russet potatoes

2 Tbsp. vegetable oil

½ cup Parmesan cheese

1 Tbsp. garlic powder

½ Tbsp. onion powder

½ Tbsp. sea salt

½ Tbsp. parsley

Directions

1. Preheat your oven to 450 degrees.

2. Peel and slice your potatoes. It is important you cut them the same size so they cook at the same rate.

3. Rinse off the potatoes and place them in a large ziploc bag. Add the oil to the bag. Seal and shake to coat the potatoes.

4. Add the remaining ingredients to the bag. Seal and shake until coated.

5. On a baking sheet or baking stone lined with parchment paper, place your coated potato slices.

6. Bake for a total of 30 minutes. Bake for 15 minutes on one side, then turn them over for the remaining 15 minutes.

7. Serve with your favorite dipping sauce.

Romantic Tip:

Sometimes changing your normal routine can spark romance. Making a new dish, using candles or mood lighting, or bringing home a bouquet of flowers to set the stage for romance... spice it up!

GARLIC PARMESAN KNOTS

These are a favorite among my friends and family. I have never shared these without someone asking for the recipe.

Ingredients

½ cup warm water (115-120°F)

1 Tbsp. olive oil

¼ tsp. sea salt

¼ tsp. sugar

1½ tsp. active dry yeast

1¼ cups flour

for the garlic coating:

1 Tbsp. olive oil

½ Tbsp. unsalted butter

2 garlic cloves, chopped

1 Tbsp. fresh parsley, chopped

fresh grated Parmesan

sea salt to taste

Directions

1. Combine the water, olive oil, sea salt, sugar, and active dry yeast in a large mixing bowl. Wait about 5 minutes to ensure that the yeast is activated. It will become frothy if activated correctly.

2. Add in the flour and mix with your hands. Move the dough from the bowl to a lightly floured work surface to shape it into a ball. Place it back into a large clean bowl, cover with saran wrap and a kitchen towel, and set it in a warm spot to proof until doubled in size (one hour with the proper warm temperature).

3. Set up your knotting station. Make sure you have prepared baking sheets ready to go. Put out a large wooden cutting board, lightly floured. Roll out your dough, and using a pizza cutter, cut the dough into strips.

 Romantic Tip:

Purchase an inexpensive calendar reserved only for romantic notes. Keep track of upcoming romantic dates and events; don't use it as your everyday calendar. Keep this calendar as a special keepsake when the year is done. On New Year's Eve, pull out the calendar and reminisce about memories from the past year together, and plan new ones for the upcoming year.

Christi Silbaugh

4. Oil your hands to keep the dough from sticking. Tie each strip into a knot (over, under, and through) and place on your prepared baking shcct until all of the knots are finished. Place the knots about an 1½ inches apart. When finished with all the dough, cover each baking sheet with a dry, thin kitchen towel, and place in a warm, draft-free spot to rise for at least one hour.

5. While the rolls are rising, prepare the garlic coating. Gently warm the olive oil, butter, and garlic in a small saucepan. Add the chopped parsley and set aside.

6. Preheat the oven to 400 degrees.

7. After the knots have doubled in size, remove the kitchen towel, brush the knots with the garlic coating, and sprinkle them with freshly grated Parmesan cheese.

8. Place the sheet pans in the oven. Bake for 12–15 minutes or until golden. These are best served warm, but are still good at room temperature.

GRILLED GARLIC AND HERB SHRIMP

These tangy shrimp are great served over rice with a fresh salad on the side.

Ingredients

1 tsp. paprika

1 tsp. minced fresh garlic

1 tsp. Italian seasoning

1 Tbsp. fresh lemon juice

⅛ cup olive oil

¼ tsp. black pepper

1 tsp. basil

1 Tbsp. brown sugar

1 lb. large shrimp, shelled and deveined

Directions

1. Whisk all the ingredients except the shrimp together in a bowl until thoroughly blended.

2. Stir in the shrimp and toss to evenly coat with the marinade. Cover and refrigerate for at least 3 hours, turning once.

3. Preheat an outdoor grill to medium-high heat. Lightly oil the grill grate and place it away from heat source.

4. Remove the shrimp from the marinade, drain the excess, and discard the marinade.

5. Place the shrimp on a preheated grill and cook, turning once, for 5–6 minutes, until they are opaque in the center. Serve immediately.

Romantic Tip:

What is the number one thing you wish your partner did for you? Well, chances are if you would like it, so would she. Pay it forward and do it for her.

HOLLANDAISE SAUCE

Gone are the days of temperamental hollandaise. This is a no worry, no hassle, and ready in 3 minutes sauce that will amp up any dish.

Ingredients

3 egg yolks

½ cup butter

2 Tbsp. lemon juice

1 dash sea salt

½ tsp. dried ground mustard

1 dash tabasco sauce (optional)

Directions

1. Separate the eggs and add the yolks to a blender. Heat the butter in the microwave or on the stove until steaming, but not boiling.

2. With the blender turned on high, very slowly stream in the hot butter. This is called tempering your eggs by slowly making them hot. Make sure the stream of butter is very small so you don't scramble the eggs.

3. Add the lemon juice, salt, mustard, and optional hot sauce. Continue to blend until thick and creamy. Serve immediately!

Romantic Tip:
Picnic at home. You don't have to leave the house to have a delicious picnic! Try having one on the living room floor, the bedroom floor, or even in your own backyard or on your balcony! Make sure you have the rug, the picnic basket, and all the right foods. Food is just a start to your romantic day for two!

IRISH SODA BREAD

Adding a little cilantro to the rolls make them look like they are decorated with clovers—the perfect addition to this Irish dish.

Ingredients

1 tsp. canola oil

2 cups flour

1 tsp. baking soda

½ tsp. sea salt

1 cup buttermilk

cilantro for garnish

Directions

1. Preheat the oven to 425 degrees.

2. Add the canola oil to a cast iron skillet or a round baking dish.

3. In a large bowl, combine the flour, baking soda, and salt. Gradually stir in the buttermilk until the dough comes together.

4. Turn the dough onto a floured surface and knead gently a few times. Form the dough into 6 round balls and press it into the prepared pan so that the dough resembles 6 hockey pucks.

5. Press one leaf of cilantro onto each roll.

6. Cover the pan. Bake for 30 minutes, covered, then remove the top pan and bake uncovered for about 10 minutes more, until the crust is dark golden brown.

 Romantic Tip:

Have a "giving" day. One of you agrees to completely give, with no expectations about what you'll get in return. From breakfast in bed to an out-of-the-ordinary treat, one of you shows your love for the other and thereby increases intimacy for both of you.

Christi Silbaugh

KUNG PAO CAULIFLOWER

Kung pao is one of my favorite flavors. Most people make it with chicken, but I find it is tastier on cauliflower. It's a lot healthier too!

Ingredients

2 tsp. soy sauce

1 tsp. rice wine vinegar

1 tsp. cornstarch, divided

¾ tsp. sesame oil

½ head cauliflower

½ Tbsp. balsamic vinegar

1 Tbsp. chicken broth

½ tsp. sugar

1½ Tbps. canola oil

5 dried red chili peppers

½ Tbsp. minced garlic

½ Tbsp. minced ginger

2 green onions, diced

peanuts for garnish (optional)

Directions

1. Mix together 1 teaspoon of the soy sauce, the rice wine, cornstarch, and ¼ teaspoon of the sesame oil and marinate the cauliflower in it for 20 minutes or more.

2. Add the remaining 1 teaspoon soy sauce, the balsamic vinegar, broth, and sugar and set aside.

3. Heat half of the canola oil in a pan over medium-high heat, add the marinated cauliflower, and sauté it until it is just about cooked to your liking and set it aside.

4. Heat the remaining canola oil in a pan over medium-high heat. Add the chilies and sauté until fragrant, about 1 minute.

5. Add the garlic and ginger and sauté until fragrant, about 1 minute.

6. Add the sauce mixture and bring it to a boil. Add the cauliflower, green onions, and peanuts, remove from the heat, and stir in the remaining sesame oil.

 Romantic Tip:

When you are with your love, make eye contact. If you don't make eye contact, you'll look bored or uninterested in them, and that's not an impression you want to give. Remember, they are just like you— everyone wants to feel like someone is interested in what they have to say!

LATKES

Latkes are traditionally served in Hanukkah cuisine. I am not Jewish, but I love how other cultures and beliefs inspire great cuisine. Potato latkes are a perfect addition to my holiday cooking. You can serve these for breakfast, brunch, lunch, or dinner.

Ingredients

2 russet potatoes, peeled and shredded

¼ cup finely chopped sweet onion

1 Tbsp. chopped fresh dill

1 Tbsp. flour

1 egg

½ tsp. sea salt

freshly ground black pepper to taste

1 Tbsp. olive oil

sour cream or Greek yogurt (optional)

Directions

1. In a bowl, add the shredded potato and onion and mix together.

2. Squeeze out any moisture using a few paper towels, one handful at a time.

3. Place the wrung-out potato and onion mixture in a large bowl. Add the fresh dill to the mixture.

4. Add the flour to lightly coat the mixture. Add the egg, sea salt, and pepper.

5. Heat the olive oil in a large sauté pan. When the oil is hot, add mounds of the potato mixture.

6. Turn the heat to medium-high. When the bottom of each latke is nicely browned, flip and brown the other side.

7. Cooking latkes over medium-high heat turns the outside a nice crispy golden brown and gives the interior a chance to cook through.

8. Drain the latkes on paper towels. Sprinkle with a bit of salt and serve with sour cream or Greek yogurt.

 Romantic Tip:
Don't forget to make your partner feel appreciated for all they do.

Christi Silbaugh

LOADED MASHED POTATO CAKES

These scrumptious potato cakes will now forever be a major comfort food addiction for me. If you like spuds, hold on to your hats!

Ingredients

2 cups cooked mashed potatoes

½ cup Colby Jack cheese, grated

¼ cup bread crumbs

¼ cup Parmesan cheese

1 Tbsp. chopped chives

1 egg yolk

canola oil (or other low saturated fat oil)

chopped bacon or bacon bits (optional)

sour cream (optional)

Directions

1. In a large bowl, mix together well all the ingredients except the oil.

2. Using your hands, scoop out generous portions of the potato mixture and shape it into patties.

3. Spray a griddle, pan, or skillet with non-stick spray and set it on the stove over high heat.

4. Cook the mashed potato patties for 4 minutes per side.

5. Serve warm with desired toppings such as chives, sour cream, and bacon bits.

Romantic Tip:
If my husband and I had it our way, we would be together 24/7. Since we live in reality and that is probably never going to happen, I like to give him things to remember me by, especially when he has to go out of town or work late. I am working on creating a little box he can take with him with pictures, his favorite music, his favorite treat, and a love note. You can keep the love alive while you are away from each other too.

OVEN-ROASTED GARLIC MUSHROOMS

A delectable side dish with rustic flavor.

Ingredients

½ lb. fresh mushrooms, whole and cleaned

2 garlic cloves, minced

1 Tbsp. balsamic vinegar

sea salt to taste

freshly ground black pepper to taste

2½ Tbsp. butter

1½ Tbsp. chopped fresh parsley

Directions

1. Preheat the oven to 425 degrees.

2. Toss the mushrooms, garlic, and balsamic vinegar in a shallow baking pan. Season to taste with salt and pepper.

3. Melt the butter and pour it evenly over the top. Roast in the oven for about 20 minutes, until the mushrooms are golden.

4. Remove the pan from the oven and sprinkle parsley on top. Serve warm.

Romantic Tip:

Instead of throwing your mate into the middle of dinner the minute he or she gets home, provide a nice appetizer and drink for them as you finish getting the meal ready. Ask them about their day while they eat this fine dish. It is just enough to awaken their palate and get themready for the main meal.

PARMESAN ROASTED CAULIFLOWER

Don't be afraid of cauliflower! It is a fabulous vegetable that takes on the flavor of what you cook it with. This dish is healthy, low calorie, but also full of flavor.

Ingredients

½ head of cauliflower

½ onion, sliced

2 thyme sprigs

3 garlic cloves, chopped

1½ Tbsp. olive oil

sea salt to taste

freshly ground black pepper to taste

¼ cup Parmesan cheese, grated

Directions

1. Preheat the oven to 425 degrees.

2. Cut the cauliflower into florets.

3. In a large bowl, toss together the cauliflower, sliced onion, thyme sprigs, garlic, and olive oil.

4. Season with kosher salt and freshly ground black pepper.

5. Place the cauliflower on a large rimmed baking dish or baking sheet.

6. Sprinkle with the grated Parmesan cheese.

7. Roast in the oven for 35–40 minutes.

8. Serve immediately.

Romantic Tip:

What little things do you do for your significant other? Oddly enough, a lot of times it is all the little things that add up to one big, happy relationship, or one very unhappy one. It can be as simple as filling up your wife's vitamin tray for her, having a cocktail waiting for her, or anything that lets her know you're thinking about her.

Christi Silbaugh

POTATO GRATIN

Why settle for boxed mixes with dehydrated potatoes when you can have the same thing, only fresh and better? If you have the skills to make a boxed mix, you have enough skills to follow this simple recipe.

Ingredients

2 russet potatoes, peeled

1 Tbsp. butter, softened

¼ cup heavy whipping cream

¼ cup whole milk

1 Tbsp. flour

3 garlic cloves, minced

½ tsp. sea salt

freshly ground black pepper to taste

½ cup sharp cheddar cheese, grated

Romantic Tip:

One of my favorite things to do is slip a love note or a card into my husband's lunch, or pocket, or car. Sometimes it takes him several hours to realize it's there, but when he does, he always calls or texts me about how grateful he is. It makes us both feel good. Give it a try with your spouse!

Directions

1. Preheat the oven to 400 degrees.

2. Smear the softened butter all over the bottom of individual baking dishes (custard cups or ramekins work great).

3. Slice the potatoes into thin slices.

4. In a separate bowl, whisk together the cream, milk, flour, minced garlic, salt, and pepper.

5. Place ⅓ of the potatoes into the bottom of the baking dish. Pour ⅓ of the cream mixture over the potatoes. Repeat this two more times, ending with the cream mixture.

6. Cover with foil and bake for 30 minutes.

7. Remove the foil and bake for more 20 minutes, or until the potatoes are golden brown and bubbling.

8. Add the grated cheese to the top of the potatoes and bake for 3–5 more minutes, until the cheese is melted and bubbly.

9. Allow the gratin to stand for a few minutes before serving.

DESSERTS

Brownies

Caramel Cheesecake Bites

Chocolate Mousse

Chocolate Pots de Crème

Chocolate Shortbread
    Thumbprint Cookies

Chocolate Toffee Rolls

Cinnamon Apple
    Quinoa Parfait

Cinnamon Rolls

Dark Chocolate Chip
    Cookies

Dark Hot Chocolate

Lava Cakes

Lemon Soufflés

Orange Dreamsicle Ice Cream

Pumpkin Streusel Muffins

Rhubarb Crisp

Salted Caramel
    Shortbread Cups

Scones

Strawberry Cupcakes

White and Dark
    Peanut Butter Cups

BROWNIES

Sometimes you just have to have chocolate. When life gives me a bad cold, bad weather, and a bad day, this is my answer.

Ingredients

1½ cups sugar

⅔ cup canola oil

¼ cup water

2 cups chocolate chips

2 tsp. vanilla extract

4 eggs

1½ cup flour

½ tsp. salt

½ tsp. baking soda

for the frosting:

¼ cup sugar

¼ cup water

3½ oz. bittersweet chocolate

1 Tbsp. vanilla extract

4 egg yolks

½ cup butter

Romantic Tip:

Write a short note to your love that is spread out over several postcards, then mail the cards one at a time. You'll build anticipation for the romantic conclusion on the final postcard, which you should deliver in person.

Directions

1. Preheat the oven to 325 degrees.

2. Combine the sugar, oil and water in a saucepan set over medium-high heat. Cook the mixture until it starts to boil. Remove from the heat. Add the chocolate chips and vanilla. Stir until the chocolate is fully melted and the mixture is smooth.

3. Mix in the eggs, one at a time, until fully incorporated. Mix together the flour, salt, and baking soda. Mix the dry ingredients, about a half cup at a time, into the chocolate mixture, mixing just until smooth.

4. Pour the batter into a prepared and greased 8 × 8 pan. Bake in the center of the preheated oven for 35–40 minutes. Remove the pan to cool completely.

5. Now make the frosting. In the top of a double broiler set over hot water, combine the sugar and water. Cook until the sugar dissolves. Add the chocolate and vanilla. Cook, mixing well, until the chocolate has melted. Add the yolks and cook, stirring constantly, until they are incorporated. Add the butter, stirring until it has melted and the mixture is smooth.

6. Pour the frosting into a container and let it sit, uncovered, until it has completely cooled. Refrigerate or freeze until it is spreadable. Spread the frosting over the cooled brownies.

Christi Silbaugh

CARAMEL CHEESECAKE BITES

Makes 12 mini cheesecake bites

This recipe went viral online, and for good reason. If you love caramel and love cheesecake, this may just be a dream come true! The secret is the amazing almond crust.

Ingredients

9 oz. cream cheese

½ tsp. vanilla extract

⅛ cup sugar

1 large egg

¼ cup sugar

1 Tbsp. water

½ Tbsp. butter

¼ cup evaporated milk

for the almond crust:

½ cup almond meal

⅛ cup slivered almonds

⅛ cup sugar

⅛ tsp. salt

⅛ tsp. ground cinnamon

⅛ tsp. baking soda

⅛ cup melted butter

Directions

1. Preheat the oven to 350 degrees.

2. In a mixing bowl, whisk together all the almond crust ingredients except the butter. Add the butter and combine with a spoon.

3. Line a muffin tin with liners. Push the almond mixture into the bottom of the liners and bake for 10 minutes to set.

4. Turn the oven down to 300 degrees.

5. In a mixing bowl, add the cream cheese, vanilla, sugar and eggs. Beat until light and fluffy.

6. Spoon the mixture into the muffin tins with the prepared almond crust.

7. Bake for 40 minutes.

 Romantic Tip:

Spend the evening playing games together—cards and board games, not video games. Get competitive!

Christi Silbaugh

8. While the cakes are cooking, start on the caramel. Combine ⅛ cup granulated sugar and 2 tablespoons water in a medium heavy saucepan over medium-high heat. Cook until sugar dissolves, stirring gently for 3 minutes.

9. Stop stirring and continue cooking for 10 minutes or until the mixture is the color of light brown sugar. Remove it from the heat and carefully stir in the butter and milk.

10. Place the pan over medium-high heat until the caramelized sugar melts. Bring it to a boil and cook 1 minute.

11. Remove the pan from heat and let the caramel cool to room temperature. Cover and chill for 1 hour or until slightly thickened.

12. Take the cheesecakes out of the oven when they are done. Once cool, the middle will slightly fall and this is the perfect indent for the caramel.

13. Spoon about 1 tablespoon of caramel over each cheesecake.

CHOCOLATE MOUSSE

This chocolate mousse is so smooth and decadent! It's definitely one of our favorites.

Ingredients

4 egg yolks

¼ cup espresso or strong coffee, room temperature

⅛ tsp salt

3 Tbsp. sugar, divided

¾ cup chilled heavy cream, divided

6 oz. semisweet chocolate (61-72% cacao), chopped

2 egg whites

Directions

1. Combine the egg yolks, espresso, salt, and 2 tablespoons sugar in a large metal or double broiler (do not allow the bowl to touch the water). Cook for about a minute, whisking constantly, until the mixture is lighter in color, has almost doubled in volume, and registers 160 degrees on a thermometer.

2. Remove the bowl from the pan. Add the chocolate and whisk until melted and smooth. Let it stand until it reaches room temperature.

3. Beat the egg whites in another medium bowl on medium speed until foamy. With mixer running, gradually beat in the remaining 1 tablespoon sugar. Increase the speed to high and beat until firm peaks form.

4. Fold the egg whites into chocolate in one at a time, then fold the whipped cream into the mixture until just blended together.

5. Divide the mousse among two 8-ounce ramekins. Chill until firm, at least 2 hours.

6. Before serving, whisk the remaining ¼ cup cream in a small bowl until soft peaks form. Dollop it over the mousse and serve.

Romantic Tip:

Create a romantic slideshow using old photos of you and your love. Sort pictures by years and events, starting from when you first met until now. Add some romantic music, then set a date for both of you to enjoy it.

CHOCOLATE POTS DE CRÈME

The creamiest chocolate custard you will ever make.

Ingredients

1 cup heavy whipping cream

3 oz. semi-sweet chocolate

½ tsp. vanilla extract

3 egg yolks

⅛ cup sugar

Romantic Tip:
Be sure to compliment your partner on something every single day. That quiet comment can be just the thing to lifts his or her spirits for the entire day.

Directions

1. Preheat the oven to 300 degrees.

2. Place four ramekins or wide-mouthed jars in large baking dish. Add the cream to a saucepan and bring it to a simmer. Remove from the heat and add the chocolate. Stir until the chocolate is melted, then add the vanilla and mix thoroughly.

3. Whisk the eggs and sugar in a large bowl until the mixture is thick and pale.

4. Drizzle a bit of the hot chocolate mixture into the eggs to temper, whisking constantly. I found it easiest to use my Kitchen Aid mixer for this.

5. Continue slowly adding the hot liquid while whisking, until all the liquid is incorporated. Avoid incorporating air into the mixture if possible. If you find you have some small unmelted particles of chocolate at the bottom of the saucepan, gently heat them until they are melted and add them to the bowl.

6. Place a fine mesh sieve over a large measuring cup and strain the custard. You may have the urge to skip this step. DON'T!

7. Pour the custard into the jars. Then pour enough hot water into pan to reach halfway up the jars. I find it easiest to use a pitcher to fill the pan so none of the water spills into the jars. Cover the pan with foil and poke a few holes in the foil to allow steam to escape. Bake for 25–30 minutes or until the outer inch of the custard is set.

8. Refrigerate until serving time.

Desserts

CHOCOLATE SHORTBREAD THUMBPRINT COOKIES

Makes 1 dozen

My two favorite things, combined into one delectable cookie.

Ingredients

½ cup + 1 Tbsp. butter, softened

⅓ cup sugar

¼ cup cocoa powder

½ tsp. vanilla

1 cup flour

¼ tsp. salt

¼ tsp. baking soda

½ tsp. baking powder

sprinkles (optional)

for the frosting:

2 Tbsp. cocoa powder

½ cup powdered sugar

2 Tbsp. hot water

½ tsp. vanilla extract

Romantic Tip:
Verbally express your admiration and respect for your love. Often.

Directions

1. Preheat the oven to 350 degrees.

2. Cream the butter and the sugar together until smooth.

3. Add the cocoa powder and vanilla extract and mix until incorporated.

4. In a separate bowl, combine the flour, salt, baking soda, and baking powder.

5. Add the dry ingredients to the butter mixture and mix until just combined.

6. Roll the dough into balls and make an indent with your thumb in the center of each ball.

7. Bake for 7–9 minutes or until the cookies are dry looking and lightly cracked on the surface, but are still very soft.

8. When they come out of the oven, press the centers down again to make a more defined well for the frosting. Allow them to cool.

9. Whisk together the frosting ingredients and spoon the frosting into the centers of the cookies. Add sprinkles, if desired.

10. Allow the frosting to set before storing the cookies in airtight containers.

Christi Silbaugh

CHOCOLATE TOFFEE ROLLS

Makes 6 rolls

Chocolate, toffee, and sweet bread. Get ready to be praised, because this dessert is out of this world!

Ingredients

¾ cup warm water

2¼ tsp. active dry yeast

½ cup sugar

1 tsp. salt

¼ cup buttermilk

⅓ cup canola oil

1 egg

4½ cups flour

for the filling:

5 Tbsp. unsalted butter

16 oz. bittersweet chocolate

8 oz. toffee bits

¼ cup sugar

for the drizzle:

4 oz. semi-sweet chocolate

¼ cup heavy whipping cream

2 Tbsp. toffee bits

Directions

1. In a large mixing bowl or the bowl of a stand mixer fitted with a dough hook, pour in the water, yeast, and 1 tablespoon of the granulated sugar. Stir and proof for 5 minutes. Once the mixture looks bubbly and frothy, pour in the remaining sugar and salt. Stir on low for 20 seconds.

2. In a small bowl whisk together the buttermilk, oil, and egg, until the egg is incorporated.

3. Pour the contents of the small bowl into the water and yeast mixture. Stir for another 20 seconds in the mixer.

4. Pour 2 cups of the flour into the mixer and stir on low until incorporated. Scrape down the sides of the bowl.

5. Sprinkle the remaining flour in by ¼ cup increments until the dough cleans the sides and bottom of the bowl. The dough should be sticky, but not sticky enough to stick to your hands when touched. Once it has reached this stage, turn the mixer back on and knead the dough for 5 minutes.

Romantic Tip:

Choose to spend a night in with your love rather than going out with the rest of your friends. Let them know you put your relationship first.

Christi Silbaugh

6. Remove the dough from bowl, grease the bowl, and place the dough back in the bowl. Cover with plastic wrap and a dish towel. Let it rise for 1–2 hours or until the dough has doubled in size. I use a heating pad on low to ensure a perfect temperature for rising.

7. While the dough is rising, chop up your chocolate and set out your unsalted butter so it will be soft by the time the dough is ready. Set aside.

8. When the dough has doubled size, punch it down. Flour a large, clean table liberally with flour. Roll the dough out into a 20 × 30 rectangle. Feel free to cut off the edges to even it all out. I save my cut-off edges and make a small serving of monkey bread with it.

9. Spread the softened butter over the dough right to the edges, leaving a 1-inch strip untouched on one of the longer sides of dough. Measure out your sugar, toffee, and chocolate and make sure it is all chopped. Add the butter and sprinkle this mixture on top of the buttered dough.

10. Roll the dough up into a tight log, finishing with the plain dough on the bottom, which you can use to seal the entire thing together.

11. Slice your rolls into 2-inch slices and place them in a well greased 11 × 13 baking dish.

12. Cover the pan with plastic wrap and dish towels. Let the rolls rise for another 1–2 hours, or until they are touching and have doubled in size.

13. Preheat your oven to 350 degrees.

14. Bake in a preheated oven for 20–25 minutes, or until the tops start to brown.

15. To make the chocolate drizzle: Melt your chocolate and whipping cream in a double broiler or microwave for 3 minutes at 50% heat. Drizzle it on top and sprinkle with toffee bits.

CINNAMON APPLE QUINOA PARFAIT
Makes 4 parfaits

Sometimes dessert can be healthy. This parfait is healthy enough to be served for breakfast, but sweet enough to be enjoyed as a dessert.

Ingredients

2 cups non-fat vanilla Greek yogurt

for the apples:
4 granny smith apples, peeled and thinly sliced

1 tsp. ground cinnamon

1 tsp. vanilla extract

2 Tbsp. sugar

1 cup water

for the oat crumble:
1 cup rolled oats

1½ Tbsp. canola oil

1 Tbsp. sugar

1 tsp. cinnamon

for the quinoa:
1 cup quinoa

2 tsp. cinnamon

2 tsp. sugar

Directions

1. Start by making the cinnamon apples. In a medium saucepan over medium heat, combine the apples, cinnamon, vanilla, sugar, and the water, mixing well. Bring the mixture to a boil and reduce the heat to low. Partially cover and cook for about 10 minutes, until the apples are softened and the liquid is syrupy. Add more water if needed during the cooking process. Take the apples off the heat and let them cool completely. Cover and refrigerate for at least 1 hour.

2. Preheat the oven to 350 degrees. Combine the oats, canola oil, sugar, and cinnamon in a small bowl. Evenly spread on a baking sheet and bake until golden brown, about 7–10 minutes. Set aside to cool.

3. Cook 1 cup quinoa according to the package directions. Once cooked, add the cinnamon and sugar and mix well. Set aside to cool.

4. Spoon ¼ cup of the yogurt into the bottom of a glass or bowl. Spoon ¼ cup quinoa on top of the yogurt. Spoon ¼ cup cinnamon apples on top of the quinoa.

5. Repeat the layering and top with the oat crumble. Repeat with the remaining glass or bowl.

 Romantic Tip:
Go to a park. Push each other in the swings and just talk.

CINNAMON ROLLS

Makes 12 rolls

If you love a good cinnamon roll, then look no further. This is my all time best cinnamon roll recipe.

Ingredients

⅜ cup warm water

1⅛ tsp. active dry yeast

¼ cup sugar

½ tsp. salt

⅛ cup buttermilk

⅛ cup canola oil

1 egg

2½ cups flour

for the filling:

¼ cup butter, softened

½ cup brown sugar

1¼ Tbsp. cinnamon

1 Tbsp. cornstarch

for the frosting:

2 oz. cream cheese

¼ cup butter

1 tsp. vanilla extract

½ Tbsp. corn syrup

1¼ cup powdered sugar

Directions

1. In the bowl of a stand mixer fitted with a dough hook, pour in the water, yeast and 1 tablespoon of the granulated sugar. Once the mixture looks bubbly and frothy, pour in the remaining sugar and salt.

2. In a small bowl, whisk the buttermilk, oil, and egg, until the egg is well incorporated. Pour the contents into the water and yeast mixture. Stir for 20 seconds in the mixer.

3. Pour 2 cups of the flour into the mixer and stir on low until incorporated. Sprinkle the remaining flour in by ¼ cup increments until the dough cleans the sides and bottom of the bowl.

4. Once it has reached this stage, turn the mixer on again and knead for 5 minutes. Remove the dough from the bowl, grease the bowl, and place the dough back in the bowl.

5. Cover the dough with plastic wrap and a dish towel. Place in a warm place. Let rise for 1–2 hours or until the dough has doubled in size.

 Romantic Tip:

The next time you're out to dinner, casually take out a pen and write a note to your love on a paper napkin—letting them know what they can look forward to at home. Fold it and slide it across the table.

Christi Silbaugh

6. In a medium size bowl, stir the butter, brown sugar, cinnamon, and cornstarch together until combined. Set aside. Punch down the dough. Flour a large, clean table liberally with flour.

7. Roll the dough out to into a 20 × 30 rectangle, moving the dough around to make sure it's not sticking to your work surface.

8. Spread the softened butter over the dough right to the edges, leaving a 1-inch strip untouched on one of the longer sides of the dough.

9. Dump the brown sugar mixture onto the the dough and spread it with your hands, creating an even layer over top of the butter, leaving that 1-inch strip of dough untouched. Roll the dough up into a tight log, finishing with the plain dough on the bottom, which you can use to seal the entire thing together.

10. Cut off the uneven ends to even out the log. Score the log every 2 inches and slice your rolls using those marks. Place the rolls into parchment lined, greased baking pans. Put 12 rolls into a 9 × 13, and the 3 remaining into a loaf pan or an 8 × 8. Cover the pans with plastic wrap and dish towels. Let the rolls rise for another 1–2 hours, or until they are touching and have doubled in size.

11. Bake in a preheated 350 degree for 17 minutes, or until the tops start to brown.

12. While the rolls are baking, whip the cream cheese and butter together. Stir in the vanilla and corn syrup.

13. Scrape the sides of the bowl and mix again. Add the powdered sugar and stir slowly until it starts to incorporate into the rest of the frosting mixture.

14. Mix on high for 5 minutes, or until the frosting starts to lighten in color. Scrape the sides of the bowl and mix again briefly.

15. Once the rolls have been removed from the oven, frost using half of the frosting. Then, after they have cooled down for a few more minutes, frost again with the remaining frosting. The first frosting will melt down into the rolls, and the second layer should stay put.

16. Serve warm.

DARK CHOCOLATE CHIP COOKIES

Makes 1 dozen

Everyone needs a tremendous chocolate chip cookie recipe. This recipe makes one dozen, just enough for you to have a few and share a few.

Ingredients

1½ cups flour

½ tsp. baking soda

¾ tsp. baking powder

¾ tsp salt

½ cup unsalted butter

½ cup brown sugar

½ cup sugar

1 egg

1 tsp. vanilla extract

9 oz. dark chocolate chips

Directions

1. Sift together the flour, baking soda, baking powder and salt into a large bowl and set aside.

2. Cream together the butter and sugars on medium speed until very light.

3. Add the egg and mix well. Add the vanilla.

4. Reduce the mixer speed to low, gradually add the dry ingredients, and mix until just combined.

5. Using a rubber spatula, fold in the chocolate chips.

6. Press plastic wrap against the dough and roll it up. Refrigerate for at least 3 hours, and up to 72 hours. If you are in a hurry, you can freeze the dough for 1 hour.

7. When the dough is ready to bake, preheat the oven to 350 degrees. Line a baking sheet with parchment paper or a non-stick baking mat.

Romantic Tip:

As he heads out the door to work, give your husband a passionate kiss. If he wants to know what it was for, tell him it's the appetizer for tonight's menu.

Christi Silbaugh

8. Slice the dough into cookie shapes and place them on your baking sheet or baking stone, leaving plenty of space in between each cookie.

9. Bake for 15–18 minutes, until golden brown and soft.

10. Transfer the cookies to a wire rack for 10 minutes, until just warm or room temperature. Repeat with the remaining dough (or keep some of the dough refrigerated for up to 3 days and bake into cookies at a later time). Store the leftover cookies in an airtight container at room temperature for up to 3 days.

DARK HOT CHOCOLATE

Chocolate is the flavor of romance. This dark hot chocolate is the perfect way to end a perfect meal.

Ingredients

1 cup whole milk

½ cup heavy whipping cream, extra for topping (optional)

3 oz. bittersweet chocolate, chopped

2 Tbsp. brown sugar

Directions

1. Warm the milk and cream in a medium saucepan over a medium-low heat.

2. Add the chocolate. Whisk until melted and combined.

3. Add the sugar and whisk until dissolved. Continue to warm the mixture for about 5 minutes, or until thick.

4. Top with whipped cream (either homemade or store bought) and serve!

Romantic Tip:

Exchange a chore for a date. Ask her to do a mundane task like picking up milk from the store. Then surprise her at the store with tickets to a movie she's been wanting to see (or tickets to anything) and whisk her away for a special date night she never saw coming.

LAVA CAKES

These lava cakes are so easy to make, and yet something is so decadent about them. Their ooey gooey inside calls to me. I am known for these delicious cakes back home in Oregon. Here is my famous recipe! Enjoy!

Ingredients

2 oz. unsweetened chocolate

¼ cup butter

½ cup powdered sugar

1 egg

1 egg yolk

2 Tbsp. corn starch

whipped cream for topping

Directions

1. Preheat the oven to 425 degrees.

2. Butter 2 custard cups and place them on a baking sheet.

3. Microwave the chocolate and butter in large microwaveable bowl for 3 minutes at 50% power. If you use full power, your chocolate will burn. Stir with a wire whisk until the chocolate is completely melted.

4. Let it cool slightly, then stir in the sugar until well blended. Whisk in the egg and egg yolk. Stir in the corn starch.

5. Divide the batter between the 2 custard cups.

6. Bake for 12 minutes. Serve warm, topped with whipped cream.

 Romantic Tip:
Serve some chocolate after dinner and make tonight's dessert incredibly romantic.

Christi Silbaugh

LEMON SOUFFLÉS

I love using fruit as decoration on a plate. These lemon soufflés make a really cute dessert that your love will remember for a long time.

Ingredients

2 lemons

1 egg

¼ cup sugar

½ Tbsp. flour

powdered sugar for dusting

Directions

1. Preheat the oven to 350 degrees.

2. Line a baking sheet with parchment.

3. Trim the tip end from a lemon so the fruit sits level. Cut the stem end one-third of the way down, making the cut parallel with bottom. Reserve the top of the lemon.

4. Hold a lemon above a sieve set over a bowl and scoop out the pulp. Squeeze the juice from the pulp and reserve. Repeat with the other lemon.

5. Place the lemon shells on your prepared baking sheet.

6. Combine the egg yolk, ⅛ cup of the granulated sugar, ⅛ cup of the reserved lemon juice, and flour in the heat-proof bowl of an electric mixer fitted with the whisk attachment. Beat the mixture on medium speed for about 3 minutes, until it becomes a pale yellow.

7. Place the bowl over a pan of simmering water. Whisk it constantly until very thick, for about 8 minutes.

 ### Romantic Tip:

Get up a few minutes earlier than usual, brush your teeth, and get back in bed and wake your love with a kiss.

Christi Silbaugh

8. Remove the bowl from the heat and return it to the mixer. Beat the mixture on medium speed until cool, scraping down sides several times, for about 10 minutes. Transfer to a medium bowl and set aside.

9. Combine the egg white and the remaining ⅛ cup granulated sugar in clean mixing bowl. Place the bowl over the pan of simmering water and stir until the sugar has dissolved and the mixture is warm to the touch. Remove the bowl from the heat and return it to the mixer. Beat on low speed until frothy. Gradually increase the speed until the meringue is shiny and holds soft peaks, for 2–3 minutes, being careful not to overbeat.

10. Whisk ⅓ of the meringue into the yolk mixture. Gently fold in the remaining meringue. Carefully fill the prepared lemon shells to just below the rims.

11. Transfer the baking sheet to the oven and bake for about 20–25 minutes, until the meringue is slightly golden and rises about 1 inch above the shell. Remove from the oven and transfer to serving plates. Garnish with the reserved lemon tops and dust with powdered sugar.

ORANGE DREAMSICLE ICE CREAM

The combination of oranges and cream make this a special treat.

Ingredients

1 cup sugar

2 cups freshly squeezed orange juice

1 Tbsp. lemon juice

1 tsp. vanilla extract

1½ cups heavy whipping cream

Directions

1. Whisk the sugar into the orange juice until dissolved, then add all the other ingredients. Pour the mixture into your ice cream maker and mix until frozen.

2. It took me 8 oranges to get 2 cups of fresh squeezed orange juice. But oh my, was it worth it! You can serve the ice cream in the empty orange skins that you have from juicing.

3. Store the ice cream in a freezer-safe container. It's a great base for a smoothie, especially with added protein powder.

Romantic Tip:

No matter what your budget is, remember to have one date night a week. Getting out together sparks conversation and rekindles romance that fades so fast in today's busy hustle-and-bustle life.

PUMPKIN STREUSEL MUFFINS

Makes 6 muffins

These are better than any other muffins I have ever had. If you like pumpkin spice, get ready for your taste buds to explode!

Ingredients

for the cream cheese filling:

2 oz. cream cheese, softened

¼ cup powdered sugar

¾ tsp. vanilla extract

for the struesel:

3 oz. chopped white chocolate

¼ tsp. cinnamon

for the muffins:

½ cup flour

1 tsp. pumpkin pie spice

¼ tsp. ground cinnamon

¼ tsp. ground ginger

¼ tsp. ground nutmeg

¼ tsp. ground cloves

¼ tsp. baking soda

¼ tsp. salt

1 egg

½ cup sugar

½ cup canned pumpkin puree

¼ cup butter

1 Tbsp. vegetable oil

1 tsp. vanilla extract

Directions

1. For the cream cheese filling: In a medium bowl, stir together the cream cheese and powdered sugar until smooth. Add the vanilla and stir to combine. Put the filling in a ziploc bag in the freezer while you prepare the muffins.

2. Preheat the oven to 350 degrees.

3. Line a muffin tin with paper liners and set aside.

4. For the streusel: In a medium bowl, use a fork to combine the chopped white chocolate and cinnamon. Set aside.

5. Whisk together the dry ingredients, from the flour to the salt, in a large bowl.

6. In a medium bowl, whisk together the remaining ingredients. Pour the pumpkin mixture over the dry ingredients and mix.

 Romantic Tip:

Find something that your significant other really likes. Maybe it isn't something you would choose, but maybe it is. You will be surprised how happy it makes you too! Finish the night out with a romantic outfit for a finishing touch!

Christi Silbaugh

7. Pour the batter into your prepared muffin pan. Using a spoon, or finger, make the center of your muffins hollow.

8. Divide the cold cream cheese mixture into each muffin.

9. Sprinkle the prepared streusel on top of each muffin.

10. Bake until golden, for 25 minutes. Cool in the pan for about 5 minutes, then remove muffins to a cooling rack to cool completely.

RHUBARB CRISP

I use sucanat for this recipe. It is pure evaporated cane juice, also called "organic brown sugar." You can use regular brown sugar, but the sucanat gives it a rich molasses flavor that my husband loves.

Ingredients

½ cup sugar

2 tsp. cornstarch

¼ tsp. cinnamon

4 cups fresh rhubarb, chopped

½ cup flour

½ cup rolled oats

½ cup sucanat

¼ tsp. salt

3 Tbsp. butter, melted

Directions

1. Preheat the oven to 375 degrees.

2. In a medium bowl combine the sugar, cornstarch, and cinnamon. Stir in the rhubarb.

3. Pour into a prepared baking dish, coated with cooking spray or parchment paper.

4. In another medium bowl combine the flour, oats, sucanat, and salt. Stir in the melted butter. Sprinkle this mixture over the rhubarb.

5. Bake for 30–35 minutes or until the fruit is tender and the topping is golden brown.

6. Serve warm.

Romantic Tip:

Pamper your love with a relaxing foot massage. All you need is a warm basin of water, some soap, a towel, and some lotion.

SALTED CARAMEL SHORTBREAD CUPS

Makes 1 dozen

These little cups of salted caramel taste like heaven. You can always use a cutter and make them look perfect, but I like the rustic homemade look.

Ingredients

½ cup + 2 Tbsp. unsalted butter

½ cup sugar

½ tsp salt

1 egg yolk

1⅔ cups flour

sea salt flakes

for the caramel:

1 cup unsalted butter

1 cup brown sugar

¾ cup light corn syrup

2 tsp. salt

4 Tbsp. sugar

4 Tbsp. heavy whipping cream

1½ tsp. vanilla extract

Directions

1. Line a baking stone or baking sheet with parchment paper.

2. In a large bowl combine the butter, sugar, and salt with a pastry cutter or fork. Add the egg yolk and continue mixing until it has a damp sand-like consistency.

3. Add the flour and use your hands to combine the dough until you can start to form shapes with it.

4. Form cups with your hands out of the dough, and refrigerate them for 30 minutes.

5. Preheat the oven to 350 degrees.

6. Use a fork to make little holes in the bottom of the chilled shortbread cups. This will keep it from breaking and flaking apart.

7. Bake for 25 minutes. Set aside to cool.

 ## Romantic Tip:

As you grow older, don't forget the happy, fun child within you. Sometimes we take on the role of a parent and forget to behave like a child now and then. Instead of feeling jealous or annoyed when your spouse acts like a child, join them and have fun!

Christi Silbaugh

8. For the caramel, combine the butter, brown sugar, corn syrup, salt, sugar, and heavy cream. Bring to a boil and stir for 5-10 minutes, until the caramel reaches the "soft ball stage" at around 230 degrees.

9. Remove from the heat, stir in the vanilla, and pour the caramel into the shortbread cups. Sprinkle with sea salt flakes and serve!

SCONES

These scones are light and fluffy on the inside with a crunchy outside layer, just as they should be.

Ingredients

2 cups flour

4 tsp. baking powder

¾ tsp. salt

⅓ cup sugar

4 Tbsp. butter

2 Tbsp. shortening

¾ cup heavy whipping cream

1 egg, beaten

sugar for sprinkling on top

Directions

1. Heat the oven to 375 degrees.

2. In a large mixing bowl, combine the flour, baking powder, salt, and sugar. Mix well.

3. Cut in the butter and shortening.

4. In a separate bowl, combine the cream with the beaten egg, then add to dry ingredients.

5. Turn the dough out onto a floured surface

6. If you have a cast iron skillet, I recommend using it. Just fill the skillet with the scone dough and bake. You can also roll the dough out, cut it into biscuit size rounds, and bake it on a baking sheet.

7. Sprinkle the dough with sugar and bake it for 15 minutes if biscuit size, 20–25 minutes in a skillet, or until brown.

 Romantic Tip:

Play twenty questions. Each of you thinks of ten questions you'd love to know the answer to. Try questions like, "If you introduced me to a stranger today, what one thing would you say that you really appreciate about me?" or "If money was not a factor, where would you like to go on a romantic getaway?"

STRAWBERRY CUPCAKES
Makes 6 cupcakes

Fresh strawberries are the secret ingredient that puts these cupcakes over the top.

Ingredients

1 cup flour
¾ cup sugar
¼ Tbsp. baking powder
¼ tsp. salt
6 Tbsp. butter
¾ cup puréed strawberries
2 egg whites
⅛ cup milk
⅓ cup fresh strawberries

for the frosting:
4 oz. cream cheese
⅛ cup puréed strawberries
⅛ cup sugar
½ tsp. vanilla extract

Directions

1. In a mixing bowl, combine the flour, sugar, baking powder, and salt. Mix on low speed for 30 seconds.

2. Add the butter and strawberry puree to the mixture and mix to blend. Then beat them for about 3 minutes, until they are light and fluffy.

3. In another bowl, whisk the egg whites and milk.

4. Add the egg whites and milk, half the mixture at a time, to the cake batter. Blend after each addition until incorporated, wipe down sides of bowl, and blend again.

5. Pour the batter into the prepared cupcake tins. Bake for 30 minutes, then set aside to cool.

6. While the cupcakes are cooking, make the frosting. With an electric mixer, beat together the cream cheese, strawberry puree, sugar, and vanilla. Chill until you are ready to frost the cakes.

7. After cakes have cooled, frost the cakes, top with fresh strawberries, and serve.

 Romantic Tip:
People have different needs when it comes to space. Some people are fine with having others around all the time, while some get annoyed when they don't have their alone time. Give each other space to be the kind of people you are individually, and you'll see that your love will blossom.

WHITE AND DARK PEANUT BUTTER CUPS

Makes 12 peanut butter cups

If you are a peanut butter fan, you are going to be thrilled with how easy it is to make this treat at home.

Ingredients

8 oz. semi-sweet chocolate pieces

½ cup creamy natural peanut butter

2 Tbsp. butter, softened

¼ cup powdered sugar

8 oz. white chocolate, chopped

Directions

1. Line a standard 12 cup muffin tin with paper cupcake liners.

2. Melt the semi-sweet chocolate, either in a double boiler or in the microwave, for 3 minutes at 50% heat.

3. Distribute the melted chocolate into the 12 muffin tins, barely filling the bottom of each cup.

4. If the chocolate does not lie flat, drop the pan repeatedly on the counter and it will flatten and smooth itself out. Place the pan in the freezer for 15 minutes.

5. In the meantime, whip the peanut butter, butter, and powdered sugar together with a hand mixer until light and fluffy.

6. Place small tablespoons of peanut butter into each cup, then drop the pan repeatedly on the counter again to help the peanut butter lie flat. Place the pan in the freezer for 15 more minutes.

 Romantic Tip:

We all have ups and downs. When you're having a bad day, walk up to your significant other, without saying a word, and just hold them tight. They will be overwhelmed with love and affection, not to mention delirious happiness because they know they're the one who makes you feel better.

Christi Silbaugh

7. Melt the white chocolate in the same way you melted the dark chocolate. Portion small spoonfuls of chocolate into the cups, one cup at a time, immediately dropping the pan repeatedly on the counter to flatten each cup. Flatten out the tops immediately after you pour the chocolate into each cup.

8. Place the peanut butter cups in the freezer for 15 minutes to set.

9. You can either refrigerate them for a peanut butter cup with more bite, or leave them at room temperature for a softer, creamier bite. Just peel the wrapper off and enjoy!

INDEX

ACKNOWLEDGMENTS

This book is dedicated to my children, who are now finding their way in the world, in hopes that they can continue to enjoy the food they grew up on, even before they have their own big families. I also want to give a big thank you to my husband, Randy, who encourages me every day, gives me honest recipe reviews, and inspires my romantic tips. Thank you to all my friends and family that support me—you all know who you are. Most of all, a big thank you to my Heavenly Father. Without Him, nothing is possible.

ABOUT THE AUTHOR

CHRISTI SILBAUGH started cooking gluten-free in 2009 when her daughter was diagnosed with Celiac disease. Since then, she has created and posted over 1,000 gluten-free recipes. Her cooking obsession and love for her family has turned a hobby into a full-time career of blogging and writing. She is the self-educated chef and author of three cooking blogs, including: *Mom, What's For Dinner, Gourmet Cooking For Two,* and *Zero Calorie Life.* She writes for foodie media giants Glam Media and Federated Media and works for Fast Forward Events, covering food and wine events in San Diego.